PHONICS WORKBOOK

COVE SCHOOL PHONICS WORKBOOK

Long Vowels

Joyce Dadouche, M.A.
Laura L. Rogan, Ph.D.
Janis Wennberg, M.A.

Cove Foundation, Winnetka, Illinois

SRA/McGraw-Hill
Columbus, Ohio

ISBN 0-02-686976-4

1 2 3 4 5 6 7 8 9 10 MAL 99 98 97 96 95 94

Contents

Sight words (to read directions) 7

Review Vowel Digraphs
  Workbook 8

Sight words (to read directions) 15

Vowel digraph **oo** 16

Two-syllable words that begin
  with **be-** or **a-** 22

Pattern words: **-o-e** with **u** sound 25

Words: **give, live, have** 26

Two-syllable words with **o** or **i** 27

Sight words (to read directions) 28

Tense endings: **-ed, -ing** 29

Vowels and consonants 32

Base words and endings 34

Review 41

Long **a** with final **e** 44

Long **i** with final **e** 58

Review long **a** and long **i**
  with final **e** 71

Endings: **-s, -es** 73

Number words 74

Long **o** with final **e** 77

Long **u** with final **e** 89

Long **e** with final **e** 102

Review long **o, u,** and **e**
  with final **e** 105

Review long **a, i, o, u,** and **e**
  with final **e** 107

Pattern words with **-ie, -oe, -ue** 113

Vowel-consonant
  combination **ow** 116

Sight words:
  who, whose, where, there 123

Review 126

Contractions with **will** 128

Two-syllable words with
  different medial consonants 130

Two-syllable words ending with
  -y, -ly, -ty 134

Contractions with **not** 143

Sight words: **what, were, said** 145

Review 147

Abbreviations: **Dr., Mr., Mrs.** 150

Adding **-ing** to words that
  end with **e** 151

Contractions with **is** and **have** 156

Pattern words with
  -old, -olk, -oll, -olt, -ost 158

Pattern words with **-ild, -ind** 160

Pattern words with endings 162

Comparative endings: **-er, -est** 164

Review of contractions 166

Review of book 168

Glossary 173

Words you will need

Read the words in each box. Do as they tell you.

A [sentence] tells. It ends with this mark [.]

Put the words into a [sentence].

cat The is big <u>The cat is big</u>.

A [question] asks. It ends with this mark [?]

Put the words into a [question].

yet you Did lunch eat <u>Did you eat lunch yet</u>?

This is a [circle]. ◯

[Circle] all the T's. (T) U V T (S) L T L Z

This is a [picture].

[Circle] all the dogs in this [picture].

He will [finish] waxing his car.

[Finish] this [picture].

[Circle] the [question].

Can he see his dog?

He can see his dog.

[Finish] the [sentence].

I see the sun in the <u>sky</u>.

shy   sky

Review

Read the words in each box. Circle the word that matches each picture.

plow / **(play)** / plea	her / hay / how	~~bay~~ / bee / **(bar)**	
(peel) / **(pool)** / pail	**(shout)** / short / **(shoot)**	pork / perk / **(park)**	
road / **(read)** / raid	**(howl)** / **(hail)** / **(heel)**	**(boost)** / boast / beast	
(boat) / beat / boot	**(store)** / **(~~steer~~)** / stair	~~port~~ / part / **(pout)**	
farm / **(fern)** / foam	car / core / **(cow)**	brown / **(brain)** / bray	

See the picture. Do the things the sentences tell you to do.

1. Put a big X on the swing on a tree.

2. Box in the dog that was in the pool.

3. Put a mark on seven flowers that are in the garden.

4. Connect the beach ball and the kitten by the tree.

5. **Box in the other kittens.**

6. Put a small ◯ under the bench.

7. Connect the children that are playing in the sandbox.

8. Put a small X next to the sailboat.

10

Review

Read the sentences. Choose the word that fits each sentence and print it in the blank.

1. He put sand in the other _bucket_ .   bucket
2. The _buckete_ on his belt was black.   buckle

3. Ray wants a _pickle_ with his sandwich.   pinker
4. This flower is _pincke_ than that flower.   pickle

5. Gail wants blue _markers_ whenever she colors.   market
6. Is the purple _marble_ under the couch?   markers
7. Mom went to the _market_ to get food.   marble

8. Greg left the _bottle_ of pop on the counter.   bottom
9. I lost a blue _button_ from my coat.   button
10. Bring the dishes from the _bottom_ shelf.   bottle

11. A needle is _sharper_ than a noodle.   sharpen
12. Dad will _sharpen_ the ax so he can split logs.   sharper

13. A tea _kettle_ hisses when the water is hot.   kettle
14. The gray _kitten_ sleeps in your chair.   kitten

15. Grandmother has a _____ on a chain.   locket
16. Jean got her lunch from her _____ .   locker

Read the question. Circle <u>yes</u> or <u>no</u>.

1. Do children ever skip on playgrounds?.................yes   no

2. Do you sprinkle salt on toast? ....yes   no

3. Can a wallet be held in your hand? ....yes   no

4. Will you limp if you sprain an ankle? ....yes   no

5. Can a butterfly be orange and black? ....yes   no

6. Are freckles ever purple? ....yes   no

7. Is it smart to cross streets in front of traffic? ....yes   no

8. Can you store things in closets? ....yes   no

9. Is yellow a darker color than blue? ....yes   no

10. Do teachers scribble on classroom walls? ....yes   no

11. Is a dozen more than seventeen? ....yes   no

12. Can a snail pull a sled uphill?.........................yes   no

13. Was a cat ever a kitten?................................yes   no

14. Is a fresh cracker crisp? ....yes   no

15. Is a task a thing that can be eaten? ....yes   no

16. Can tweezers get splinters out of your skin? ....yes   no

17. Is your father taller than you? ....yes   no

18. Do children ever act in school plays? ....yes   no

19. Is three inches longer than six inches?.................yes   no

20. Can we mix black and white to get the color gray? ....yes   no

Review

Read the sentences. Choose the word that fits each sentence and print it in the blank.

1. Mom put salt and _____ on the roast.	puppet
2. If I pull the strings, my _____ walks.	pepper
3. I need more _____ for my bedroom closet.	handles
4. He _____ that brown and white horse well.	hangers
5. The rich man has a maid and a _____ .	butter
6. The farmer fed the horse a _____ of hay.	butler
7. He says he wants _____ on his popcorn.	bundle
8. Mom put a yellow _____ in the playpen.	racket
9. Another _____ apple fell on the ground.	rattle
10. Dad got a tennis _____ from the store.	rotten
11. Chimps at the zoo are from the _____ .	jumper
12. My mother is pressing my orange _____ .	jungle
13. To leave trash on the ground is to _____ .	letter
14. We drop a _____ into a mailbox.	litter
15. The small dog needs a _____ collar.	little

Review

Choose a word from the box and print it on the blank line next to the thing you need it for.

soap	fork	rain	green
hammer	mittens	leash	white
patches	hay	raft	
boots	flour	racket	

1. to fix torn jeans: _____

2. to color the leaves on a tree: a _____ marker

3. to put on your hands in winter: _____

4. to eat your dinner: _____

5. to clean the dishes: _____

6. to feed horses: _____

7. to color clouds in the sky: _____ paint

8. to pound a nail into a board: _____

9. to keep flowers in the yard blooming: _____

10. to put on your feet when it is wet: _____

11. to mix with eggs and milk for waffle batter: _____

12. to walk your dog: _____

13. to float on water: _____

14. to play tennis: _____

Review

Read the sentence. Choose the letter pair you need to finish the word.
Print the letters in the blank.

1. Glen and I will each pass out tr _____ ts to the class.
   ea ai

2. R _____ pushes his blue truck up the little hill in the park.
   ay ag

3. Blue jays swoop d _____ n to get the seeds near the tree.
   ow ar

4. Do you want Mother to paint your r _____ m this color?
   oa oo

5. Three buttons fell off your gr _____ jacket.
   ab ay

6. Ann shreds the swiss ch _____ se to put in the blender.
   ee oo

7. I was helping Father push the shopping c _____ t.
   ar oa

8. Rabbits nibble on the plants in our back y _____ d.
   ai ar

9. My mother will get a yellow and white quilt f _____ my bed.
   ee or

10. We kept our swimming p _____ l up all summer long.
    ee oo

11. Miss Finch prints with white chalk on the chalkb _____ rd.
    oa ea

12. Was the n _____ l in your coat pocket?
    ai ow

13. They want an orange ch _____ r to match the couch.
    ee ai

14. I am going to color the cl _____ n with a purple marker.
    ea ow

15. After school, Jill rushes to the p _____ k to play ball.
    or ar

16. I help squ _____ ze oranges for drinks to go with a snack.
    ee ou

More words you will need

Read the words in each box. Do as the words tell you.

To draw is to

Draw a box.

This is a line . _____

Put a line under this box.

To write is to

Write a word. _____

We can put a puzzle together .

Circle the puzzle that is put together .

To remember is to not forget.

Do you remember which seat is yours?

Draw a tree.

Write 2 words.

_____

Draw lines to connect the letters.

A

B

C

D

E

To not forget is to

_____ .

-oo- as in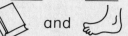

When you see **oo,** you say the sound you hear in <u>boot</u> and <u>food</u>.

Another sound for **oo** is the sound you hear in 📖 and 🦶 .

Draw a line from the letters to the pictures that have the **oo** sound

as in 📖 .

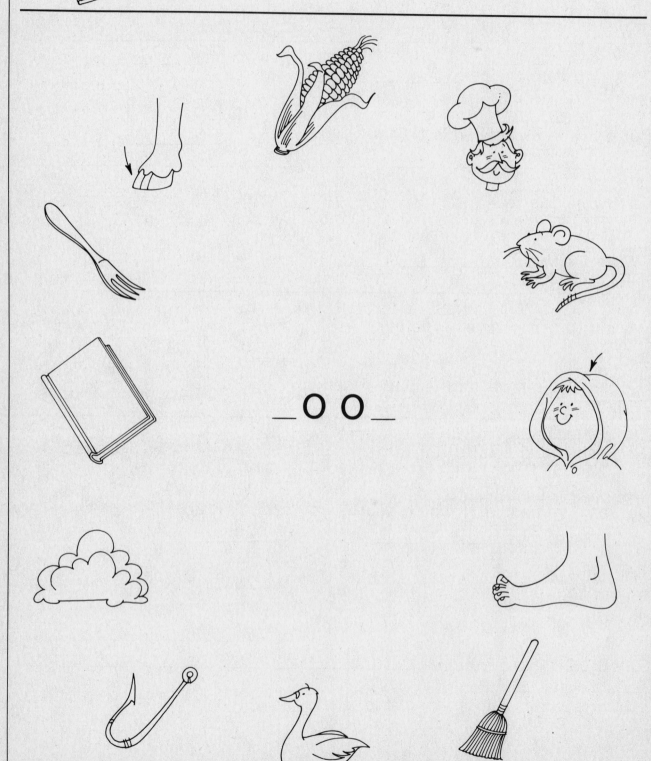

-oo- as in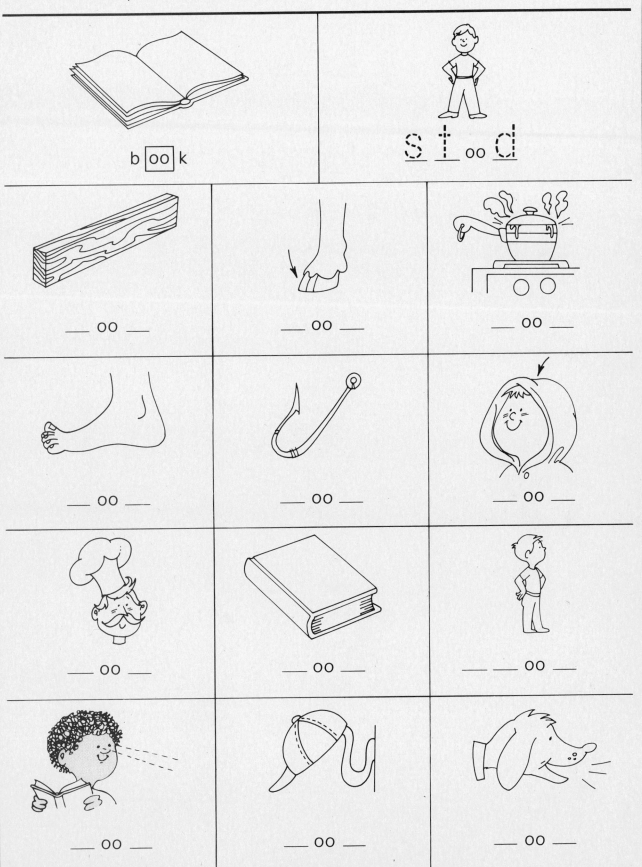

Look at the picture. Say the word. Fill in the missing letters.
Look at the sample to see how to do it.

b oo k

s t oo d

__ oo __

__ oo __

__ oo __

__ oo __

__ oo __

__ oo __

__ oo __

__ oo __

___ oo __

__ oo __

__ oo __

__ oo __

-oo- as in ▢

Look at the picture. Say the word. Choose the letter or letter pair
you need to finish the word. Look at the sample to see how to do it.

sh OO k	dr ____ p	t ____ k
o oo	o oo	o oo

bl ____ ck	br ____ k	r ____ ck
o oo	o oo	o oo

r ____ d	w ____ l	l ____ k
o oo	o oo	o oo

st ____ p	w ____ f	sh ____ t
o oo	o oo	o oo

st ____ d	cl ____ ck	fl ____ ck
o oo	o oo	o oo

Two sounds of -oo-

Look at the pictures and the words in each box. Draw lines to connect the words to the pictures.

coop	brook	good
cook	broom	goose
took	stoop	loop
tool	stood	look
book	hoop	cook
boot	hoof	cool
food	shoot	hoot
foot	shook	hook

Two sounds of -oo-

1. Write the words with the **oo** sound in <u>boot</u> on the lines under <u>boot</u>.
2. Write the words with the **oo** sound in <u>book</u> on the lines under <u>book</u>.

---

pool   hood   good   shook   smooth   look   soon   tooth

oo ⟶ boot	oo ⟶ book

1._____   1._____

2._____   2._____

3._____   3._____

4._____   4._____

Read the sentences. Fill in the correct word.

cook   foot   took   stood   hood
cool   food   tool   stool   hoot

1. Never pester Mom when she is trying to _____ dinner.

2. Help me rinse the mud off the garden _____s.

3. Go get the kitchen _____ and put it next to the chair.

4. Last month it was too _____ out to go swimming.

5. Mom says you must put the _____ up on your jacket.

6. Tell Al to quit snacking on the _____ in his lunch box.

7. My _____ is too big to squeeze into that little boot.

8. If you go into the woods, you may hear an owl _____.

9. She _____ the ladder and put it next to the shelves.

10. The children _____ by the shrubs in front of the house.

-oo-

Read the sentence. Choose the correct word. Write it on the line.

1. You see stars when you _____ up into the dark sky.
   look   lock

2. In the spring we go for long walks in the _____.
   woods   woofs

3. Mom wants us to eat good _____ so we will be strong.
   foot   food

4. If the cars do not _____, they will crash into each other.
   stood   stop

5. Scott has to keep a _____ on his locker at school.
   lock   look

6. We _____ off our jackets and hats when it got hot.
   took   tock

7. Dad _____ on a ladder when he was cleaning the gutters.
   stood   stop

8. The food that Mom is cooking for dinner smells _____.
   good   goat

9. Glen puts on _____ if he wants to splash in puddles.
   boots   books

10. Miss Speck was _____ for another book for me.
    locking   looking

11. My little brother _____ his rattle in his playpen.
    shock   shook

12. I swept the leaves off our porch with a _____.
    broom   brook

13. That _____ coat scratches me whenever I put it on.
    wheel   wool

14. He has no _____, so he cannot fix the leg on my desk.
    took   tools

15. Miss Camp wants us to hang up our coats on the _____.
    hooks   hoots

16. Ray held my _____ for me as I put on my coat.
    booths   books

Words that begin with be- and a-

Read the words at the top of each box. Read the sentence at the bottom of the box. Circle the word you need in the sentence. Look at the sample to see how to do it.

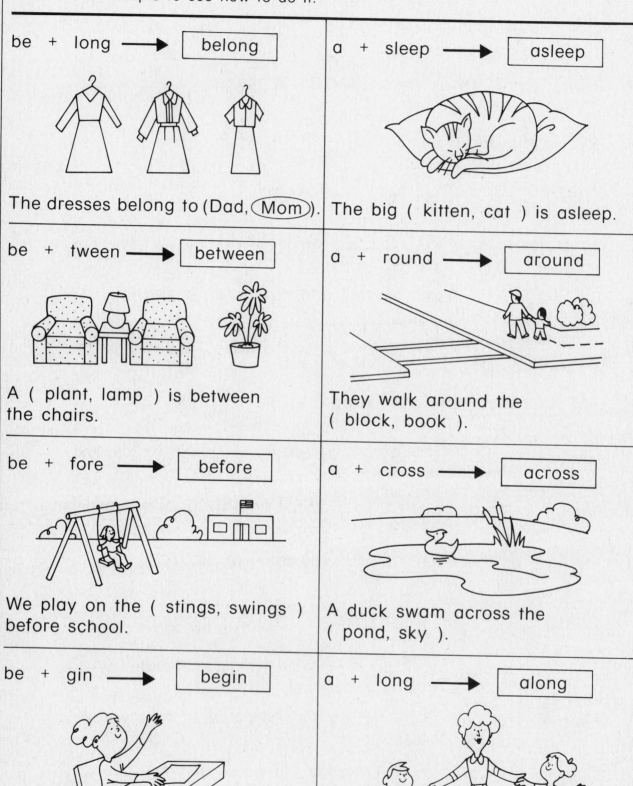

be + long → belong

The dresses belong to (Dad, (Mom)).

a + sleep → asleep

The big (kitten, cat) is asleep.

be + tween → between

A (plant, lamp) is between the chairs.

a + round → around

They walk around the (block, book).

be + fore → before

We play on the (stings, swings) before school.

a + cross → across

A duck swam across the (pond, sky).

be + gin → begin

Ann needs (help, fun) to begin.

a + long → along

Mom went along with (us, park).

Words that begin with **be-** and **a-**

Read the words. Print the letters on the lines.

before is be•fore

afraid is __ • __ __ __ __ __

between is __ __ • __ __ __ __ __

away is __ • __ __ __

apart is __ • __ __ __ __

belong is __ __ • __ __ __ __

Fill in the word that belongs in the sentence.

1. Today we will see another good film _____ rockets.
   about   away

2. I took the sharp stick _____ from my little brother.
   away   apart

3. After lunch our teacher reads books _____ to us.
   belong   aloud

4. I put rubber bands _____ the pens in my desk.
   aloud   around

5. I put on my jacket with the hood _____ I go out.
   before   after

6. The sky was full of clouds before it _____ to rain.
   began   again

Words that begin with **be-** and **a-**

Read the words. They all begin with **a-** or **be-**. Circle the **a-** or **be-**.

---

began	**a**part	**be**fore	**a**round
ago	**be**tween	**a**gain	**a**fraid

Fill in the blanks. Choose the words you need from the top.

1. My cat is _____ of thunderstorms.

2. I got a kitten from a pet store a month _____ .

3. If you bump that puzzle, it may fall _____ .

4. Dad took us to the zoo _____ last Sunday.

5. Mom says we can split the popcorn _____ us.

6. The big crowd _____ to cheer for the team.

---

begin	**a**long	**a**part	**be**long
asleep	**a**bout	**a**loud	**a**way

---

7. We ran _____ the path under the trees.

8. Our teacher asks us to read _____ from our books.

9. The paints and brushes _____ to my sister.

10. A farm with a brook is not far _____ from our house.

11. The sky is so dark I think it will _____ to rain.

12. Grandmother tells us _____ things she did when she was little.

some	done	none	come	gloves	above

Read the sentences that tell about the pictures.

Mom is cooking roast beef.
Sam wants some .

Jean is cleaning out her desk.
Pat is all done .

Joan took out three books.
Bev took none today.

We are going to look for shells.
Kay will come along with us.

Look, you can see the moon!
It is above the trees.

Al has a pair of wool mittens.
Jeff has cotton gloves .

Read the questions. Fill in <u>yes</u> or <u>no</u>.

1. Will Kay go to the beach? _____

2. Will Sam eat some roast beef? _____

3. Did Bev get more books than Joan? _____

4. Was Pat still cleaning out her desk? _____

5. Is the moon above the trees? _____

6. Can gloves ever be cotton? _____

give	live	have

Read the sentence that tells about the picture. Next, read the sentences with blanks in them. Fill in the blank with the correct word.

Fish live in the water.

Rabbits live in the _____ .   farm

Children live in _____ .   woods

Goats and cows live on a _____ .   coop

Chickens live in a _____ .   houses

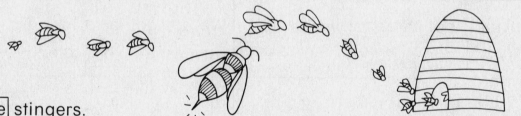

Bees have stingers.

Cars have _____ .   wings

Apples and oranges have _____ .   wheels

Pigs have _____ .   seeds

Eagles have _____ .   snouts

Cows give us milk.

Clouds give us _____ .   wood

Plants give us _____ to eat.   rain

Trees give us _____ for chairs.   food

Sheep give us _____ for gloves.   wool

Longer words with **i** and **o**

Read the sentences that tell about the pictures. See how the words in the boxes end with **-en, -er,** or **-el.** This will help you read them.

A cook put muffins in the oven .

Mom will cover him with a sheet.

I have a sliver in my finger.

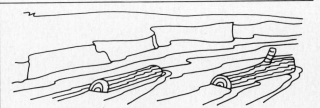

Some wood is floating in the river .

He began to shiver in the rain.

Dad digs with a shovel .

Finish the sentences. Write the correct word on the line.

shiver   liver   river   sliver   oven   cover   shovel

1. Mother began cooking some food in the _____ .

2. We have fun going down the _____ in our boat.

3. Mom says that _____ is good for us to eat.

4. I put a _____ on my paints when I am done.

5. When you get a chill, you may _____ .

6. I need tweezers to get a _____ out of my finger.

7. I went along to watch the men dig with the steam _____ .

More words you will need

Read the words in each box. Do as the words tell you.

The rabbit in the middle is different .

Draw another flower that is different .

This is a page in a book.

Put an X on the page with a picture.

She hung the small pictures
 below the big painting.

Put an X on the big painting.

This stick is short.   These sticks are long.

Put an X on the long sticks.

He got all wet because it was raining.

Put an X on Al.

He is by the base .

Put an X
on a
base.

Word endings -ed, -ing

A word + **ing** means something is happening now.
A word + **ed** means something did happen before.

When you see ed, say "Ed."

Fill in <u>yes</u> or <u>no</u>.

> **ing** means now
> **ed** means before

NOW    → **BEFORE**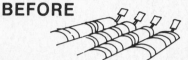

We are plant **ing** a garden.

Are we plant **ing** seeds?

We plant **ed** all the seeds.

Did we plant the seeds?

_____

 →

It is melt**ing** in the sun.

Is the hot sun melt**ing** it?

It melt**ed** in the sun.

Did it melt in the cool wind?

_____

 →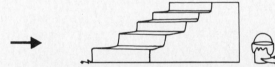

He is paint**ing** the porch.

Is he paint**ing** the roof?

He paint**ed** the steps gray.

Did he paint the steps green?

_____   _____

 →

Mom is braid**ing** her hair.

Is Tom braid**ing** her hair?

Mom braid**ed** her hair.

Did Mom braid her hair?

_____   _____

They are load**ing** the truck

Are they load**ing** the truck?

They load**ed** the truck.

Did they load the truck?

_____   _____

When you see **ed** on this page, say "d" or "t."

Fill in <u>yes</u> or <u>no</u>.

ing = now
ed = before

NOW   **BEFORE**

They are play **ing** checkers.   They play **ed** before dinner.

Are they play **ing** chess?   Did they play after dinner?

_____   _____

He is jump**ing** into the pool.   They all jump**ed** into the pool.

Is he jogg**ing** in the pool?   Did they jump into the pool?

_____   _____

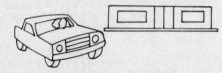   

Mom is park**ing** the car.   Mom park**ed** by the store.

Is Mom sitt**ing** in the car?   Did Mom get out of the car?

_____   _____

We are watch**ing** TV.   We watch**ed** TV in my room.

Is the TV set on?   Was the TV on the porch?

_____   _____

Mom is dress**ing** Scott.   Cliff dress**ed** himself.

Is Dad dress**ing** Scott?   Did Mom dress Cliff?

_____   _____

Word endings -ed, -ing

Finish the words with **-ing** or **-ed**. Circle <u>now</u> or <u>before</u> to tell if something is happening now or if it happened before.

1. They are clean**ing** up the playroom.   (now)   before

2. Mark count_____ all his cash before he left.   now   before

3. They all jump_____ off the porch and ran.   now   before

4. I think my little sister must be dream_____.   now   before

5. Jill wash_____ her hair after school today.   now   before

6. He hammer_____ nails into the loose board.   now   before

7. I think Bill trick_____ me yesterday.   now   before

8. Mom shorten_____ my wool slacks last week.   now   before

9. Tom is print_____ letters on the chalkboard.   now   before

10. Dad butter_____ the muffins for us this morning.   now   before

11. Please tell your dog to quit bark_____ .   now   before

12. It was so hot we all want_____ a drink.   now   before

13. We flatten_____ the big boxes yesterday.   now   before

14. Beth and Don are sweep_____ the leaves off.   now   before

15. Our house was paint_____ white last summer.   now   before

Read this. Circle the correct word.

It (was, is) dark when it stormed this afternoon. We (sit, sat) in the den and watched TV. Then we (got, get) out the checkers and played. The storm ended before we (go, went) to sleep.

Vowels and consonants

A E I O U are <u>vowels</u>. (**Y** can be a vowel or a consonant.)

Print the <u>vowels</u>: _____ _____ _____ _____ _____ (_____)

All the other letters are <u>consonants</u>.

Print the <u>consonants</u>:

_____ _____ _____ _____ _____ _____

_____ _____ _____ _____ _____ _____

_____ _____ _____ _____ _____ _____

_____ _____ _____ _____ _____ _____

1. In <u>some words</u>, **y** can do the job of a <u>vowel</u>, as in <u>fly</u> and <u>sky</u>.
   In other words, **y** can do the job of a <u>consonant</u>, as in <u>yard</u> and <u>yes</u>.
2. All the words we read <u>must</u> have a vowel. Some words have 2 or 3 vowels.

Box in the vowels in each word. Print them on the line.
Keep vowel pairs together.

b[a]g [a]_____   p[ai]nt [ai]_____   snail_____   stop_____   glass_____

shrimp_____   try_____   look_____   dry_____   float_____

next_____   treat_____   seem_____   me_____   boot_____

Vowels and consonants

Print the ABCs. Draw a circle around the vowels: **a e i o u** and **y.**

_____

—— —— —— —— —— ——

—— —— —— —— —— ——

—— —— —— —— —— ——

—— —— —— —— —— ——

Your teacher will help you read this next part.

1. When you <u>say</u> the ABCs, you say the <u>letter names</u>.

   When you <u>read</u> words, you say the <u>letter sounds</u>.

2. You make <u>vowel sounds</u> with your <u>voice</u> alone.

   You make <u>consonant sounds</u> with help from your <u>lips</u>, <u>teeth</u>, and

   <u>tongue</u>. Say some letter sounds and feel yourself make the sounds.

   t   f   a   p   m   i   g   u

_____

Count the vowels in each word. Print the words on the correct lines.

do	soap	speck	porch	cry
paint	snore	dishes	buckle	kitten
pound	scratch	steam	horse	shook

I vowel	2 vowels together	2 vowels apart
do	paint	snore
____	____	____
____	____	____
____	____	____

Base words and endings

The words you start with before you put on endings are called <u>base words</u>.

Add **-s, -ed, -er, -ing.** Read all the words with endings.

print

| p r i n t | s |

play

toast

clean

Box in the consonants.

U   Z   B   I   E   H   T   A   O   K   P   G   M

Base words and endings

Add **-en** to these base words.

Beth has eat __ __ all her oatmeal.

Has Mark beat __ __ the waffle batter for lunch?

Frank needs to short __ __ the sleeves on his jacket.

Add **-s, -ing, -ed, -er, -en,** or nothing at all to the base word.

We are eat_____ roast chicken for dinner. Father eat_____ the dark meat. Mother will eat_____ some white meat. Jan is not a big eat_____. After she has eat_____, she will go out to play.

Scott is a basketball play_____. He play_____ on the school basketball team. Last week they play_____ the Bobcats. Today they will play_____ Jackson School. Scott began play_____ last year.

Beth has an egg beat_____. She beat_____ three eggs for the waffles. After the eggs are beat_____, she mixes them with some flour. She thinks beat_____ eggs is fun to do!

In the morning, Mom cuts muffins and toast _____ them in the toast _____. I can smell them toast _____ when I go into the kitchen. I eat the toast _____ muffins with peanut butter and jam.

Twin consonants in the middle of longer words

These words have <u>twin consonants</u>. Fill them in!

ba __ __   The twin consonants are __ __ .

cu __ __   The twin consonants are __ __ .

ki __ __ en   The twin consonants are __ __ .

sli __ __ er   The twin consonants are __ __ .

---

1. Split these words between the <u>twin consonants</u>.
2. Write the base word on the line.

pat|ting   pat   plugged _____   spinning _____

sitting _____   clipper _____   grabbed _____

slapped _____   winning _____   shopping _____

flatten _____   popper _____   petted _____

Read the words. Fill in the <u>twin consonants</u>.

drop__ed   slip__er   shut__er   bat__ed

drop__ing   slip__ed   shut__ing   bat__er

drop__er   slip__ing   swim__ing   bat__ing

Add the twin consonant, then:

Add **ing** to <u>drop</u> to get drop p i n g .

Add **ed** to <u>drop</u> to get drop__ __ __ .

Add **er** to <u>drop</u> to get drop__ __ __ .

1. Fred kept drop__ __ __ __ his pens off his desk.

2. When Jan drop__ __ __ her schoolbag, all her books fell out.

Add the twin consonant, then:

Add **ing** to <u>slip</u> to get slip__ __ __ __ .

Add **ed** to <u>slip</u> to get slip__ __ __ .

Add **er** to <u>slip</u> to get slip__ __ __ .

1. Meg slip__ __ __ her boots off her feet.

2. Pat puts her blue slip__ __ __s on her feet.

1. Split the words between the twin consonants to get the <u>base</u> words.
2. Write the base word on the line.

bat|ting bat   sledding _____   splitting _____

grinning _____   quitting _____   shutter _____

chipped _____   chopped _____   skipped _____

38

Base words

Box in the base words.
Keep **-ck, -ch,** or **-sh** together with the base word.

-ck	-ch	-sh
picked	hitching	rushed
sticker	richer	wishing
clicking	pinched	splashed

Read the sentence. Circle the word you need to finish each sentence.

1. Dad was (snapping, sanding, snatching) wood to get it smooth.

2. We counted as the rocket (blasted, blotted, boasted) off.

3. I (plugged, played, plucked) the cord into the other socket.

4. Fran was (pinned, picked, pinched) to be a cheerleader again.

5. The orange (rubber, runner, richer) ball belongs to my sister.

6. Al is a (duster, dropper, drummer) in the school band.

7. Our dog is (sticking, stitching, sitting) between us.

8. I (plucked, plugged, played) on the swings yesterday.

9. She got her left (slipper, sticker, slicker) from the closet.

10. Three children are (stacking, standing, stamping) next to me.

Base words that end with -le

Hint: When you want to add **-ed** or **-er** to words that end with **-le,** leave out one of the **e**'s.

Add **er** to <u>dribble</u> to get _____ .

Add **ed** to <u>dribble</u> to get _____ .

1. Pam is the best _____ on our basketball team.

2. Today she _____ the ball past Mark and Liz.

Add **ed** to <u>sprinkle</u> to get _____ .

Add **er** to <u>sprinkle</u> to get _____ .

1. Dad _____ the dry grass yesterday.

2. Tim ran under the spray from the _____ .

Add **ed** to <u>puzzle</u> to get _____ .

Add **er** to <u>puzzle</u> to get _____ .

1. The teacher asked a question that _____ me.

2. That riddle was a real _____ .

Box in the base word. Print the letters of the base word on the lines.
Keep **-le** with the base word.

1. We get juggler from _____ .

2. We get saddled from _____ .

3. We get waffles from _____ .

4. We get sparkler from _____ .

5. We get crumbled from _____ .

Base words that end with -le

1. Choose the word you need to finish each sentence.
2. Write the word on the line.

puzzles   puzzled

1. Beth took a box of _____ down from the shelf.

beagles   beagle

2. The dog that Ann got for a pet is called a _____ .

bubble   bubbled

3. Ken wanted to have some of your _____ gum.

juggle   juggler

4. My big brother is a good _____ .

puddles   puddle

5. Gail stepped in a _____ and got her feet all wet.

buckles   buckled

6. Jack got in the back seat and _____ his seat belt.

pickled   pickles

7. Jill took some dill _____ with her sandwich.

scrambled   scrambles

8. I think I will have some _____ eggs for lunch.

sample   sampled

9. We got a little _____ of soap from the store.

sparkles   sparkler

10. Look how that star _____ in the sky.

1. Read the sentence.
2. Circle yes if the sentence tells about something that can happen.
   Circle no if the sentence tells about something that never happens.

---

1. We went swimming each day at summer camp. ....yes   no

2. Pebbles are softer than cloth. ....yes   no

3. Tom batted in three runs for his team. ....yes   no

4. We see puddles in the street when it is dry. ....yes   no

5. I stamped the dishes and dropped them
   in the mailbox. ....yes   no

6. The children scrambled the puzzles before
   they started. ....yes   no

7. Pat stumbled and dropped all her bundles. ....yes   no

8. Jan giggled when she watched the clown.........yes   no

9. Dad planted the bottles with a shovel............yes   no

10. The rain trickled down and tickled my neck. .....yes   no

11. The farmer planted cornstalks in the barn.........yes   no

12. We watched the loud thunder as it rumbled. .....yes   no

13. White is a darker color than gray. ....yes   no

14. My father snores when he sleeps. ....yes   no

15. The cars crashed into each other
    at the corner. ....yes   no

16. The fish stopped running down the beach. ....yes   no

Review

Read each sentence. Read the endings for the sentence that is not finished.
Put an X on the line next to the best ending.

Dan lost his lunch box. He looked all around and then found it—

_____ above the roof of his house.

_____ beneath the rug on the stairs.

_____ in back of the clock on the wall.

_____ next to his school books.

It was cool when Ann went to bed. Mom covered her with a—

_____ pair of wool gloves.

_____ blanket for a doll.

_____ quilt that belonged to her grandmother.

_____ cover to the toaster.

Jim was looking for the best spot to keep his book. He will put it—

_____ along the shrubs in the backyard.

_____ among the dishes in the kitchen sink.

_____ between some bookends on his dresser.

_____ beneath his twin bed.

Jill got a little kitten from the pet shop. She needs something soft
to put in the bottom of the box for her kitten. The best thing is—

_____ some scraps of wood.

_____ a torn cotton sheet.

_____ a thick and stiff braided rug.

_____ a rubber raincoat.

Do this crossword puzzle with the words at the top of the page.

cookbook   garden   bookshelf   fish   belongs   winter
bleachers   trunk   hot dog   dry   oven   kitten

Across

2. I put on gloves in the ____ .

6. After a bath you will ____ off.

7. You read this before you cook.

8. This will be a cat some day.

9. If it is yours, it ____ to you.

12. We watch football from the ____ .

Down

1. This is put in a bun.

3. The back of a car has a ____ .

4. Dad began to dig in the ____ .

5. You keep books on a ____ .

10. The roast is in the ____ .

11. It lives in a river or brook.

a words that end with -e

When you see **a,** you say the sound you hear in <u>cat</u> and <u>man</u>. Another sound for **a** is the sound you hear in and . Look at all the pictures. Connect each picture that has the **a** sound as in with the letters in the middle of the page.

_a_e

a words that end with **-e**

Look at the word parts on this page. Do they all have the letter **a** in them? ______ Do they end with the letter **e**? ______ You say the letter name for the **a** in these words. Why? Because they are short words that end with **-e.** Fill in the consonants to finish these words.

cape

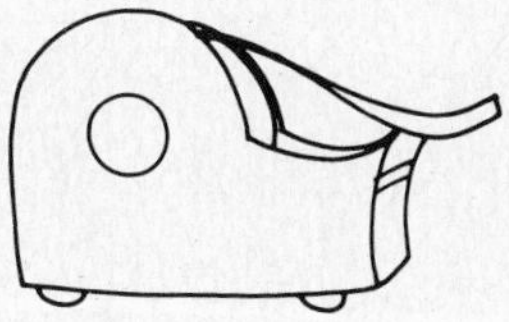

__ape

__ __ape

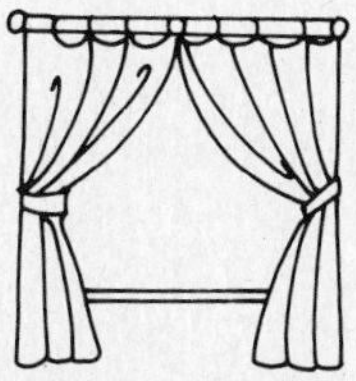

__ __ape

__ake

__ __ake

__ake

__ake

__ade

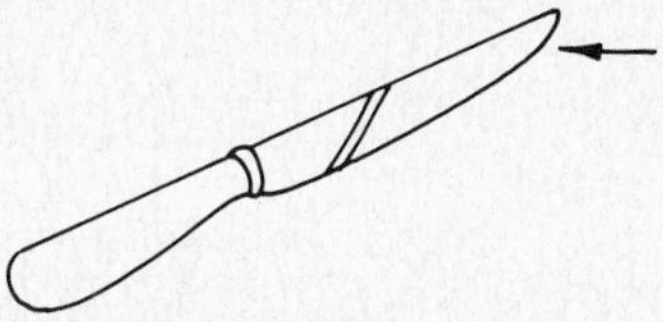

__ __ade

__ __ade

__ __ane

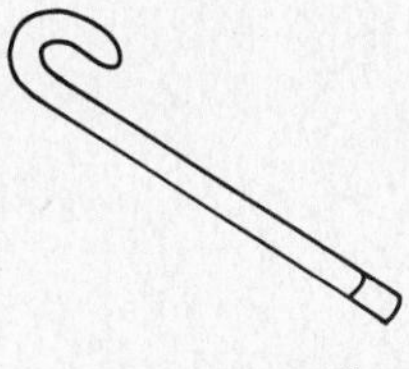

__ane

__ane

a words that end with **-e**

Circle the words that end with **-e.** Connect all the words to the correct pictures.

bake	stack	cane
back	stake	can
van	bale	taste
vane	ball	tack
mane	snack	rat
man	snake	rake
cap	shake	paste
cape	shack	pack

a words that end with -e

Look at the pictures. Then fill in the missing letters.

Fill in **e** or **d.**

bal ___   bal ___

Fill in **e** or **t.**

cas ___   cas ___

Fill in **e** or **t.**

plan ___   plan ___

Fill in **e** or **t.**

pan ___   pan ___

Fill in **e** or **s.**

van ___   van ___

Fill in **e** or **p.**

scal ___   scal ___

Fill in **e** or **t.**

sal ___   sal ___

Fill in **e** or **p.**

lam ___   lam ___

a words that end with -e

The **a** in these words sounds just a little different from the **a** in <u>cake</u> or <u>plane</u>. Look at the pictures. Fill in **a** and **e** to finish these words.

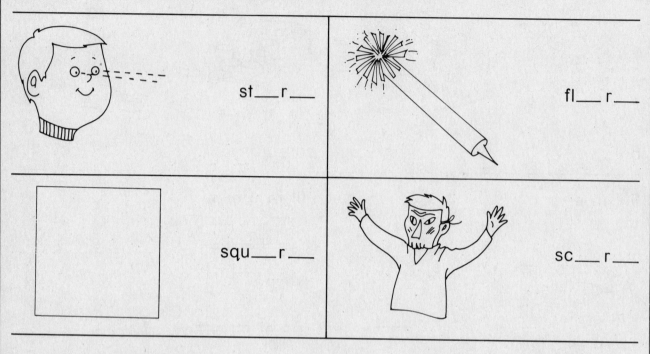

st___r___

fl___ r___

squ___r___

sc___ r___

Read these words. Then read the sentences. Fill in the blanks with these words.

rare	care	hare	square	ware
share	bare	mare	fare	scare

1. That shape on the board is round and this is _____.

2. Dad asked the waiter for his roast beef to be _____.

3. A rabbit can be called a _____.

4. If you let me play with your ball, you _____.

5. They are paying the _____ on the bus.

6. The tools you want are at the hard_____ store.

7. A loud sound can _____ you.

8. When will you take _____ of the fish tank?

9. The tree branches are _____ of leaves in winter.

10. A horse can be called a _____.

a words that end with **-e**

Fill in the blanks with the word part that you need.

Fill in with **-ack** or **-ake.**

1. I hung the r_____ up on the r_____ with the shovel.

2. Mom went b_____ to the kitchen to b_____ a cake.

3. Please t_____ a t_____ out of the box for me.

4. Do you think the sn_____ wants a little sn_____?

Fill in with **-an** or **-ane.**

1. The lame man c_____ walk better with a c_____ .

2. Dad will pl_____ to take the pl_____ to Maine.

3. The m_____ has a horse with a long m_____ .

4. I need a p_____ of water to wash this p_____ of glass.

Fill in with **-ar** or **-are.**

1. See her st_____ at that big st_____ .

2. He will take good c_____ of his sports c_____ .

3. If you go f_____ in a plane, you pay a big f_____ .

One thing or more than one?

Fill in the blanks to make the words match the pictures.

RICK

Jake Don
Matt Pat

1 name

4 nameS

 ___ ape

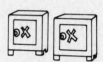 ___ ape___

___ gate

___ gate___

___ safe

___ safe___

Read and add **-s** if you need it.

a big wedding cake___

a shelf of game___

a jar of paste___

three milk shake___

a truck full of crate___

a dark cave___

Pick a bunch of grape___ .

She trade___ .

They all share___ .

Stack the plate___ .

We are brave___ .

I want a pair of skate___ .

Box in that part of the word that means <u>one</u> thing.

plates	plants	shakes	games
grapes	skates	crabs	names
crates	traps	shacks	cracks

a words that end with **-e**

Circle the correct word for the picture in each box. You can box in the base word if you need to. Remember: If a word ends with **-e**, keep **e** with the base part.

(bake|s) / back|s	whales / walls	panes / pans
quacks / quakes	plans / planes	scats / skates
cares / cars	hats / hates	grabs / grapes
drags / drapes	makes / masks	waves / waxes
flashes / flakes	scrapes / scraps	tacks / takes

Adding endings to words that end with -e

Remember: When you want to add **-ed** or **-er** endings to words that end with **-e**, leave out one of the **e**'s.

Add **ed** to <u>scrape</u> to get __ __ __ __ __ __ __.

Add **er** to <u>scrape</u> to get __ __ __ __ __ __ __.

Add **s** to <u>scrape</u> to get __ __ __ __ __ __ __.

1. Dad has a _____ with a long handle.

2. This morning Dad and I _____ the frost off the car.

3. When it is winter, he _____ the frost off the car.

Add **s** to <u>shape</u> to get __ __ __ __ __ __.

Add **ed** to <u>shape</u> to get __ __ __ __ __ __.

1. The children cut out square and round _____ .

2. We _____ the ground beef into neat meatballs last Sunday.

Add **s** to <u>wade</u> to get __ __ __ __ __.

Add **ed** to <u>wade</u> to get __ __ __ __ __.

1. Last summer, we _____ in the water looking for shells.

2. Our little sister cannot swim yet, so now she _____ near the shore.

Add **-ed** or **-er**.

1. He rock____ the boat.

2. He is a fast skate____ .

3. My dog is a loud bark____ .

4. Dad back____ up the car.

5. She rake____ the leaves.

6. Mom bake____ a cake.

7. She is a good dressmake____ .

8. I need a purple mark____ .

Adding endings to words that end with -e

Remember: When you want to add **-ed** or **-er** endings to words that end with **-e,** leave out one of the **e**'s.

Add endings to the base words to make different words.

___

My little brother can do more things each day.

We are trying to teach him to wave.

Last week we wave_____ to him as we left for school.

Now my little brother wave_____ to us whenever we leave.

___

Mom gave us popcorn with melted butter to share.

Jim went to the kitchen and got the salt shake_____ .

When he eats popcorn, he shake_____ a lot of salt on it.

___

Bill wants to trade baseball cards.

Each day he trade_____ them at school.

Yesterday he trade_____ seven of them with me.

We call him Trade_____ Bill.

___

Dad wants to keep his nails in jars.

He asked Mom to save some jars for him.

When we eat up all the peanut butter, Mom save_____ the jars.

Last week Mom save_____ three jars for Dad.

He says Mom is a good save_____ .

___

Dad has to go to the hardware store to get another rake.

Each fall he rake_____ all the leaves in our yard.

Last year we rake_____ leaves together on three afternoons.

a words that end with -e

Box in the base word. Print the letters of the base word on the lines.

1. We get ⬛ bake ⬛ r from b̲a̲k̲e̲ .

2. We get w h a l e s from __ __ __ __ __.

3. We get s c a r e d from __ __ __ __ __.

4. We get t a m e d from __ __ __ __.

5. We get s h a d e d from __ __ __ __ __.

6. We get g r a d e d from __ __ __ __ __.

7. We get s q u a r e s from __ __ __ __ __ __.

8. We get s h a v e r from __ __ __ __ __.

Read the sentence. Fill in the missing part of the word.
Choose it from the words at the bottom of the page.

1. It is a game you play with a ball and a bat.   _____ball

2. We eat them with milk in the morning.   corn_____

3. It can fly in the air.   air_____

4. It has shelves to keep books on.   book_____

5. They lived long, long ago in caves.   _____men

6. They are round and you fry them.   pan_____

7. You put it on your toothbrush.   tooth_____

8. We say that something made by hand is   hand_____

| made | plane | case | cave |
| base | cakes | flakes | paste |

a words that end with **-e**

Read these words. Do they all end with **-e**? _____ Do they all have
the vowel **a** in the middle? _____ Write the word that begins with **a**. _____

skate	take	paste	scrape
rake	grape	ape	plane

Box in the base words.
If a word ends with **-e,** keep **e** together with the base word.

Keep **e** with the base word		Keep **e** with the ending	
takes	raked	tacked	trainer
skates	grapes	panted	barked
baker	skated	planter	packed
taken	baked	backed	cashed
scraper	skater	catcher	mashes

Circle the word that belongs in the sentence.

1. Jim (skipped, skated, scatter) across the rink today.

2. She cuts and (pastes, pants, pats) in her book at school.

3. Joan (barked, backed, baked) a cake this morning.

4. Our dog (grapes, grabs, grades) the stick and runs with it.

5. Dad and I (racked, rocked, raked) the leaves in the yard.

6. Six (planes, plans, plants) began to take off at the airport.

7. Bob (tacks, takes, tasks) his lunch along with him to school.

Three ways to write the same sound

Write the words that have an **a** that sounds like the **a** in

pl ay   n ai l   c a k e

a → play
a → nail
a → cake

1. _____

2. _____

stacks	make	3. _____
waste	cracker	4. _____
planned	name	5. _____
gray	rattles	6. _____
scraps	pains	7. _____
crash	trade	8. _____
trainer	staying	9. _____
scrape	grab	

To get the base word in these words,
take off the ending and put the **e** back on.

-ed

named is name + ed   maker is make + er

traded is _____ + ____   trader is _____ + ____

scraped is _____ + ____   scraper is _____ + ____

a words that end with **-e**

Read the sentence. Choose the correct word. Write it on the line.

1. Jane held our _____ when we went on our sleds.
   skates scats

2. Todd helped when Dad _____ frost off the car.
   scraped scrapped

3. Clerks put apples on _____ before they tell what
   scalds scales
   they cost.

4. Mom will give me corn _____ and milk this morning.
   flakes flacks

5. A duck in a pond _____ at the kids watching it.
   quaked quacked

6. Glen jumped into the _____ and swam around the raft.
   lack lake

7. Miss Cook pulls the screen down before we _____ watch
   cane can
   a film.

8. The twins are _____ they will be going fishing.
   glad glade

9. Ann _____ a house from blocks she kept in her closet.
   mad made

10. Mom puts Jake in his crib so he will _____ a nap.
    take tack

11. Brad gives us salt to put on popcorn for a _____ .
    snack snake

12. Bumble bees buzzed by flowers in my _____ yard.
    back bake

13. My brother _____ when he sits by Dad in the car.
    became behaves

i words that end with -e

When you see **i,** you say the sound you hear in <u>six</u> and <u>big</u>. Another sound for **i** is the sound you hear in 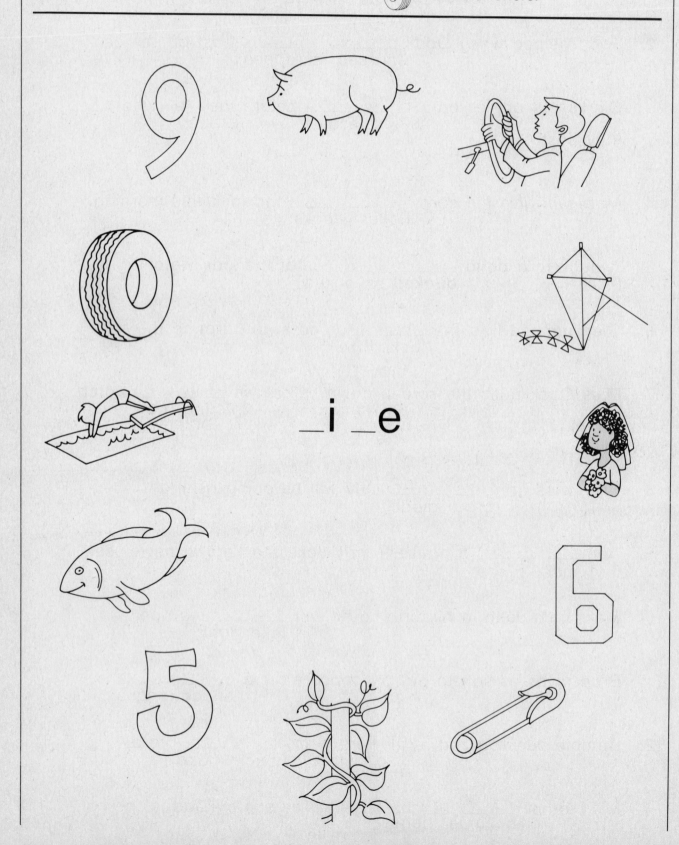 and . Look at all the pictures. Connect each picture that has the **i** sound in with the letters.

_i _e

i words that end with -e

Look at the word parts on this page. Do they all have the letter **i** in them? _____ Do they end with the letter **e**? _____ You say the <u>letter name</u> for the **i** in these words. Why? Because they are short words that end with **-e**. Fill in the consonants you need to finish these words.

h ive   __ __ ile

___ ive   ___ ile

___ ive   ___ ile

__ __ ive   ___ ile

___ ire   __ __ ide

___ ire   ___ ide

___ ire   __ __ ide

i words that end with -e

Circle the words that end with **-e.** Connect all the words to the correct pictures.

file	limp	twin
fill	lime	twine
pin	win	spine
pine	whine	spin
pile	whip	kite
pill	wipe	kit
shin	mint	slid
shine	mine	slide

i words that end with **-e**

Fill in the missing letters.

Fill in **e** or **t.**

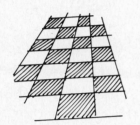

til____

til____

Fill in **e** or **s.**

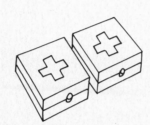

kit____

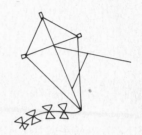

kit____

Fill in **e** or **s.**

strip____

strip____

Fill in **e** or **p.**

lim____

lim____

Fill in **e** or **s.**

pin____

pin____

Fill in **e** or **l.**

pil____

pil____

Fill in **e** or **t.**

min____

min____

Fill in **e** or **s.**

twin____

twin____

i words that end with -e

Fill in the blanks with the word part you need.

Fill in with **-in** or **-ine.**

1. The tw_____s needed tw_____ for arts and crafts class.

2. Our dog will w_____ if he does not wh_____.

Fill in with **-im** or **-ime.**

1. T_____ has a watch that helps him tell t_____.

2. I will give h_____ a d_____ for that blue pen.

Fill in with **-ip** or **-ipe.**

1. The bag is so full of r_____ apples that it may r_____.

2. The p_____ will dr_____ if you do not fix it.

Fill in with **-ill** or **-ile.**

1. Jane w_____ read a book wh_____ I watch TV.

2. The windm_____ is a m_____ away from our house.

3. Miss Crane will f_____ the f_____s for her boss.

Fill in with **-ike** or **-ick.**

1. My dog l_____s to l_____ my hand whenever I give her treats.

2. M_____ made a n_____ in the desk with his pen.

Fill in the blanks to make the words match the pictures.

___ dime

___ dime___

___ pipe

___ pipe___

___ vine

___ vine___

___ line

___ line___

Read and add **-s** if you need it.

a steep slide___

a grape vine___

five tire___

put in a pile___

a pocket full of dime___

seven mile___

Cut and squeeze some lime___ .

The dress has stripe___ .

Hear all the chime___ .

She smile___ at the little children.

They hide___ in the bushes.

We stood in the short line___ .

Box in that part of the word that means <u>one</u> thing.

stripes   miles   slips   piles

pills   pipes   lines   miles

vines   chins   strips   slides

i words that end with **-e**

Circle the correct word for the picture in each box. You can box in the base word if you need to. Remember: If a word ends with **-e**, keep **e** with the base part.

piles (pills)	wipes whips	fins fines
tins tires	bikes bills	miles mills
slides slips	wins wires	licks likes
files fills	trikes tricks	strips stripes
chins chimes	kites kits	dims dimes

Adding endings to words that end with -e

Remember: When you want to add **-ed** or **-er** endings to words that
end with **-e**, leave out one of the **e**'s.

Add **er** to <u>time</u> to get __ __ __ __ __ .

Add **s** to <u>time</u> to get __ __ __ __ __ .

1. Mom sets the _____ when she cooks eggs.

2. She _____ how long they need to be cooked.

Add **ed** to <u>smile</u> to get __ __ __ __ __ __ .

Add **s** to <u>smile</u> to get __ __ __ __ __ __ .

1. My sister _____ at me when I look in her crib.

2. She _____ at me yesterday morning, too.

Add **s** to <u>drive</u> to get __ __ __ __ __ __ .

Add **er** to <u>drive</u> to get __ __ __ __ __ __ .

1. My dad is a truck _____ .

2. He _____ a big truck each day.

Add ed or er.

1. Jane hike____ three miles.

2. He honk____ the horn.

3. We like____ the cake.

4. The cat lick____ the milk.

5. He has a smooth glide____ .

6. Dave wipe____ the counter.

7. Dad wash____ the car.

8. The farmer milk____ cows.

Adding endings to words that end with -e

Remember: When you want to add **-ed** or **-er** endings to words that end with **-e,** leave out one of the **e**'s.

Add endings to the base words to make words with other meanings.

Jeff likes his van to shine.

On Sundays he waxes and shine_____ it whenever he can.

Last Sunday he shine_____ it and went for a long ride.

The coach needs to see how fast his team can run.

He time_____ his runners. His stopwatch is his time_____ .

He starts his time_____ and watches them run around the track.

Last week he time_____ the runners six times.

After she ate her food, the kitten lick_____ up all her milk.

She like_____ the cream Mom gave her last weekend.

I think she like_____ milk better than water.

James Jackson is a bus drive_____ .

Each morning he drive_____ bus 202 on Main Street.

He never drive_____ on Greenleaf Street.

He likes to be the drive_____ of a bus.

Each spring Dan hike_____ along the trails beside the river.

Last spring he took a long hike.

He hike_____ for ten miles. He is a strong hike_____ .

i words that end with -e

Box in the base word. Print the letters of the base word on the lines.

1. We get ⬚wipe⬚d from w i p e .

2. We get rider from ___ ___ ___ ___ .

3. We get strikes from ___ ___ ___ ___ ___ ___ .

4. We get glider from ___ ___ ___ ___ ___ .

5. We get tired from ___ ___ ___ ___ .

6. We get tribes from ___ ___ ___ ___ ___ .

7. We get bikes from ___ ___ ___ ___ .

8. We get diver from ___ ___ ___ ___ .

9. We get smiles from ___ ___ ___ ___ ___ .

10. We get hiked from ___ ___ ___ ___ .

Read the sentence. Fill in the missing part of the word.
Choose it from the words at the bottom of the page.

1. It is yellow and sweet to eat.   _____apple

2. It is big and red and goes to fires.   _____truck

3. We can roast hot dogs outside on this.   camp_____

4. It is a bug that flickers in the dark.   _____fly

5. We can park the car in this.   _____way

6. We can walk or ride our bikes on this.   _____walk

7. Dad chopped the logs and made this.   wood_____

8. Bees buzz in and out of this.   bee_____

fire	pile	drive	hive
fire	pine	side	fire

i words that end with -e

Read these words. Do they all end with **-e**? _____ Do they all have the vowel **i** in the middle? _____

file	ripe	ride	stripe
like	fine	kite	trike

Box in the base words.
If a word ends with **-e,** keep **e** with the base word.

Keep **e** with the base word		Keep **e** with the ending	
filed	rides	tricked	billed
stripes	liked	filler	thriller
driver	rider	sticker	linked
striped	widen	filled	tilled
ripen	fined	licked	wilted

Circle the word that belongs in the sentence.

1. My dog (liked, licked, linked) my hand after I fed him.

2. Her blouse has green and white (stripes, strips, sticks).

3. Jake (rids, rides, rips) a bus to school each day.

4. Jeff (licks, likes, links) to ride his bike around the block.

5. Mom (filed, failed, filled) the pitcher with some orange pop.

6. My sister (fails, files, fills) her finger nails.

Two ways to write the same sound

Write the words that have a vowel that sounds like the **y** or **i** in

sk y   f i v e

y or i → five
→ sky

wish   slide   1. _____

why   slim   2. _____

dime   dive   3. _____

strips   fly   4. _____

sizzles   stripe   5. _____

pins   tire   6. _____

shine   tripped   7. _____

pine   swimming   8. _____

                       9. _____

To get the base word in these words,
take off the ending and put the **e** back on.

-ed   **-er**

timed is time + ed   wiper is wipe + er

dived is _____ + _____   timer is _____ + _____

wiped is _____ + _____   diver is _____ + _____

i words that end with -e

Read the sentence. Choose the correct word. Write it on the line.

1. We put string on our _____ so they will fly up in the sky.
   kites   kits

2. I _____ to play in my sandbox outside in the sunshine.
   like   lick

3. My short sleeved blouse has purple _____ on it.
   stripes   strips

4. Jane will come with me to pick big _____ red apples
   rip   ripe
   off the tree in the backyard.

5. Kate liked to _____ the pockets of her winter jacket with junk.
   file   fill

6. Mom wants to put the flowers she _____ in a blue vase.
   picks   pikes

7. Miss Smith can give us a lesson on how to tell _____
   time   Tim
   from the big clock in our room.

8. When the _____ in the grill is hot, the chicken gets crisp.
   fin   fire

9. Ed took Dad along to help pick out a good baseball _____.
   mitt   mite

10. I cannot wait to take a _____ of that cupcake.
    bit   bite

11. I _____ the spoon after Mom had mixed the cake frosting
    licked   liked
    with it.

12. _____ slept in our car all the way to the lake.
    Tim   Time

a and **i** words that end with **-e**

Read the words beside the picture. Connect the correct word to the picture.

time	fare	bake
tame	fire	bike

vine	like	whale
vane	lake	while

square	mane	wide
squire	mine	wade

pale	pine	hive
pile	pane	hare

lane	lime	tale
line	lame	tile

a and **i** words that end with **-e**

Read the words. Make a good sentence from the words and write it on the line.

Dave   this

lake

likes

1. _____

brook   the

Wade   across

wide

2. _____

has

Mine   white

mane   the

3. _____

Kate   kite

has   a

4. _____

The   between

the   lanes

line   is

5. _____

Mike   footprints

makes   some

6. _____

Adding -s or -es endings

When you add **-s** to a word, it means:
1. There is more than one thing.
2. Something happens again and again.

Read these words. Add **-s** if you need it.

three book___   he whistle___   it sparkle___   six mile___

a cook___   ten grape___   she play___   can howl___

he clean___   a rake___   he dive___   I score___

1. When a word ends with **-ss, -x, -zz, -ch,** or **-sh,** add **-es.**
2. Read the words. Add **-s** or **-es.**

Add **-s**	Add **-es**
dollar ___	buzz ___
toast ___	pitch ___
trick ___	splash ___
pickle ___	scratch ___

Getting the base word

1. To get the base word, you take off **-es** and add **-e.**

chases is _____ + _____   prizes is _____ + _____

grazes is _____ + _____   closes is _____ + _____

rises is _____ + _____   uses is _____ + _____

2. To get the base word, you take off **-es.**

buzzes is _____ + _____   crutches is _____ + _____

branches is _____ + _____   pushes is _____ + _____

crashes is _____ + _____   splotches is _____ + _____

Number words

Read these number words.

1	2	3	4	5	6	7	8	9	10
one	two	three	four	five	six	seven	eight	nine	ten

Connect the words with the numbers that mean the same thing.

9	one	two	2
5	five	eight	7
1	four	three	3
4	nine	seven	8

Print in the number word.

We have: _____ ears _____ mouth _____ shins

_____ neck _____ arms _____ cheeks

_____ feet _____ waist _____ chin

_____ legs _____ hands _____ back

_____ heels _____ lips _____ chest

Print in the number word.

Dogs have: _____ ears _____ mouth _____ neck

_____ legs _____ tail _____ back

Count. Print in the number word.

_____ _____ three _____ five _____

seven _____ _____ _____

Number words

Fill in a number word to finish each sentence.

1	2	3	4	5	6	7	8	9	10
one	two	three	four	five	six	seven	eight	nine	ten

1. The number between seven and nine is _____ .

2. A jacket can have _____ hood and _____ sleeves.

3. Joan had two balls. She gave _____ to me and kept _____ .

4. The number before three is _____ .

5. Two dimes and two dimes are _____ dimes.

6. None and one is _____ .

7. Dale is seven now, so next year he will be _____ .

8. A horse has _____ legs and _____ ears.

9. A bike has _____ wheels and _____ seat.

10. A car has _____ steering wheel.

11. A square has _____ sides.

12. One pair of gloves means _____ gloves.

13. One, _____, three, _____, five, six, seven, _____ .

14. Our class has eight children, so they need _____ books.

15. An armchair has _____ legs and _____ seat.

16. After seven comes _____ .

Number words

Read the sentence. Fill in the correct word.

1. If you have one cupcake and you eat one cupcake,

   you have _____ left.
   one   no   none   on

2. If you have no dimes and a pal gives you a dime,

   you have _____ dime.
   one   no   none   on

3. If James gives all his marbles to his brother,

   James will have _____ left.
   one   no   none   on

4. If Mom wants to keep the food in the pot hot,

   Mom will put a cover _____ the pot.
   one   no   none   on

5. If you have one kite and your dad gets you another kite,

   you have _____ kites.
   two   to   too   out

6. If Dave has a blue jacket and Jeff gets the same color jacket,

   then Jeff has a blue jacket _____.
   two   too   out

7. If you are not going into the store,

   you are going _____ of the store.
   two   to   too   out

8. Mom wants Todd to get her some milk.

   She is sending Todd _____ the store.
   two   to   out

9. Jane is adding in her math class.

   When she adds two and one, she gets _____.
   three   tree   the

o words that end with -e

When you see **o**, you say the sound you hear in <u>box</u> and <u>hot</u>. Another sound for **o** is the sound you hear in [bone] and [rope]. Look at all the pictures. Connect each picture that has the **o** sound as in [bone] with the letters in the middle of the page.

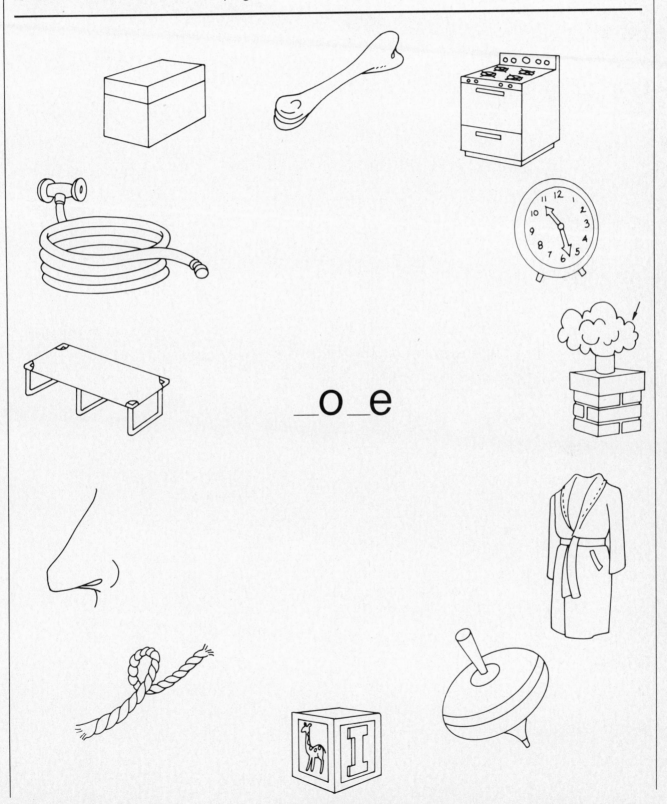

_o_e

o words that end with -e

Look at the word parts on this page. Do they all have the letter **o** in them?
_____ Do they end with the letter **e**? _____ You say the letter name for
the **o** in these words. Why? Because they are short words that end with **-e.**
Fill in the consonants to finish these words.

____one

____one

____ ____ ____one

____ose

____ose

____ose

____oke

____ ____oke

____obe

____ ____obe

____ome

____ome

____ole

____ole

o words that end with -e

Circle the words that end with **-e.** Connect all the words to the pictures.

rob	sole	hope
robe	sob	hop
Ross	froze	pot
rose	frost	pole
globe	smock	rode
glad	smoke	rod
hot	spoke	code
hole	spot	cod

80

o words that end with -e

Do these words all have **o** in them? _____ Do they all end with **-e**? _____
Read the words and connect them with the pictures.

robe

rope

hope

hole

cone

core

hose

home

doze

dome

stone

stove

pole

poke

nose

note

bone

broke

store

stole

rose

rode

sole

sore

One thing or more than one?

Fill in the blanks to make the words match the pictures.

___ mole   ___ mole___   ___ rope   ___ rope___

___ stone   ___ stone___   ___ dome   ___ dome___

Read and add **-s** if you need it.

the kitchen stove ___   He tells a joke___.

two rubber hose ___   Dogs like to hide bone___.

a classroom globe ___   Dig seven small hole___.

a vase of rose ___   She left a short note___.

a pile of stone ___   Dave rushes home___.

two fishing pole ___   Today the school close___.

Box in that part of the word that means <u>one</u> thing.

globes	flocks	hoses	bones
words	domes	gloves	frogs
notes	stoves	closets	roses

o words that end with -e

Circle the correct word for the picture in each box. You can box in the base word if you need to. Remember: If a word ends with **-e,** keep **e** with the base part.

mops / mopes	bonds / bones	hopes / hops
stoves / stops	comes / cones	pokes / pots
totes / tots	moles / mobs	smokes / smocks
stones / stomps	closes / closets	rods / robes
dozes / dozens	stores / storks	spokes / spots

Adding endings to words that end with -e

Remember: When you want to add **-ed** or **-er** endings to words that end with **-e**, leave out one of the **e**'s.

Add **s** to <u>hose</u> to get __ __ __ __ __ .

Add **ed** to <u>hose</u> to get __ __ __ __ __ .

1. We _____ the car down with water before we washed it.

2. Dad keeps the two yard _____ next to the garden tools.

Add **s** to <u>stroke</u> to get __ __ __ __ __ __ .

Add **ed** to <u>stroke</u> to get __ __ __ __ __ __ .

1. My pet kitten loves it when someone _____ her back.

2. The dog across the street likes to be _____ , too.

Add **ed** to <u>vote</u> to get __ __ __ __ __ .

Add **er** to <u>vote</u> to get __ __ __ __ __ .

Add **s** to <u>vote</u> to get __ __ __ __ __ .

1. Mom and Dad went together and _____ yesterday.

2. Someone that votes is called a _____ .

3. After we have the _____ in one pile, we will count them.

Add **-ed, -en,** or **-er.**

1. Mom joke____ with me.

2. Stand close____ together.

3. Mike honk____ the horn.

4. The lake is froze____ .

5. The golf____ looked around.

6. The blue line is crook____ .

7. Her rocker is wood____ .

8. The dishwasher was broke____ .

Adding endings to words that end with **-e**

Remember: When you want to add **-ed** or **-er** endings to words that end with **-e**, leave out one of the **e**'s.

Add endings to the base words to make words with other meanings.

My grandfather likes to smoke ribs.

He smoke_____ ribs every day at his diner.

Yesterday he smoke_____ ribs at our house.

In the hall outside his classroom Jeff has a lock_____ .

He put a lock on the handle.

After he takes his lunch out of the lock_____ , he lock_____ it.

Yesterday Matt lock_____ it for him.

We close the gate before we let our dog outside.

Each day Dad close_____ the gate after he drives the car in.

Mom close_____ the gate when my brother was in the yard.

The word doze means to sleep.

My father often doze_____ in his chair while he watches TV.

Yesterday he doze_____ off at 8:00, before my bedtime!

All the classes at school vote to choose the school colors.

I vote_____ for our colors to be purple and white.

Some of our teachers will count all the vote_____ next week.

o words that end with -e

Box in the base word. Print the letters of the base word on the lines.

1. We get rope s from r o p e .

2. We get closer from ___ ___ ___ ___ ___ .

3. We get stoves from ___ ___ ___ ___ ___ .

4. We get thrones from ___ ___ ___ ___ ___ ___ .

5. We get choked from ___ ___ ___ ___ ___ .

6. We get pokes from ___ ___ ___ ___ .

7. We get voter from ___ ___ ___ ___ .

8. We get stroked from ___ ___ ___ ___ ___ .

Read the sentence. Fill in the missing part of the word.
Choose it from the words at the bottom of the page.

1. This is a book that notes are kept in.   _____book

2. This will become a frog someday.   tad_____

3. Flags are hung outside on this.   flag_____

4. A rose bush may have this on it.   _____bud

5. This is another word for your spine.   back_____

6. Someone that wishes to be back home feels   _____sick

7. This may be found on a pine tree.   pine_____

rose   pole   bone   cone   home   pole   note

o words that end with -e

Read these words. Do they all end with **-e**?_____ Do they all have the vowel **o** in the middle?_____

slope	froze	joke	stroke
note	code	smoke	tone

Box in the base words.
If a word ends with **-e**, keep **e** with the base word.

Keep **e** with the base word		Keep **e** with the ending	
strokes	sloped	frosted	stronger
dozed	joked	stocked	tossed
frozen	broken	golfer	longer
dozes	closer	docked	looked
stroked	joker	honked	stomped

Circle the word that belongs in the sentence.

1. Mom gave me a (not, note, noted) for Grandmother.

2. Thick, black (smock, smokes, smoke) rose from the fire.

3. The short note was printed in a (cod, code, codes).

4. The hill (slope, slop, slopes) down to the lake.

5. We like to play (joked, jokes, joker) on our big brother.

6. Gail (stroke, stocked, stroked) the soft kitten in her lap.

Three ways to write the same sound

Write the words that have the letter sound of **o** as in

n $\boxed{\text{o}}$ g $\boxed{\text{oa}}$ t   b $\boxed{\text{o}}$ n $\boxed{\text{e}}$

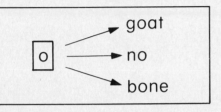

close	pond	1. _____
cost	float	2. _____
soaked	so	3. _____
socked	bottle	4. _____
broke	joke	5. _____
robs	flock	6. _____
vote	robber	7. _____
go	coat	8. _____
		9. _____

To get the base word in these words,
take off the ending and put the **e** back on.

voted is <u>vote</u> + <u>ed</u>   joker is <u>joke</u> + <u>er</u>

closed is _____ + ____   voter is _____ + ____

joked is _____ + ____   closer is _____ + ____

o words that end with -e

Read the sentence. Write the missing word on the line.

1. That big rabbit _____ faster than that little frog.
hoped   hopped

2. Before she _____ the kitchen tile, Mom fills the pail with
mopes   mops
soap and water.

3. He _____ he can have the crates filled with oranges.
hops   hopes

4. Mike took four glasses of _____ out to his pals.
pop   pope

5. Two children _____ brown horses along the wide trail.
rode   rod

6. The campfire _____ in the rain.
smoked   smocked

7. Dad will put a steel _____ up in my closet so I can
rode   rod
hang up some of my things.

8. Miss Ott makes us put on _____ before we paint.
smokes   smocks

9. When she wakes up, she will put on her yellow _____.
robe   rob

10. Dad is _____ playing golf this Sunday afternoon.
not   note

11. Do you think a man can lift a _____ of bricks alone?
tone   ton

12. Miss Swift took out the _____ to teach the class.
globe   glob

u words that end with -e

When you see **u**, you say the sound you hear in <u>duck</u> and <u>cut</u>. Another sound for **u** is the sound you hear in [cube] and [tube]. Look at all the pictures. Connect each picture that has the **u** sound as in [cube] with the letters in the middle of the page.

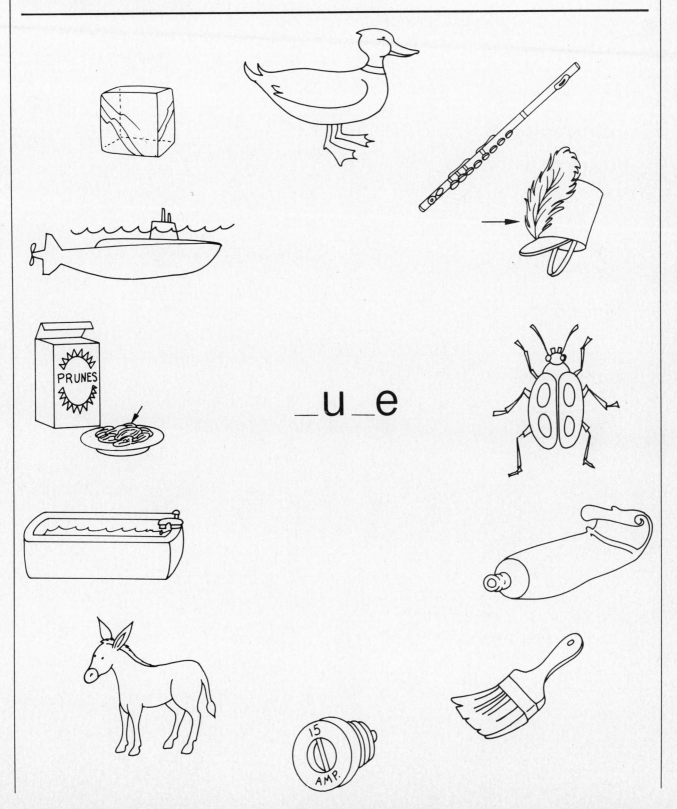

_u_e

u words that end with -e

Circle the words that end with -e. Connect all the words to the pictures.

tub	rule	luck
tube	run	Luke
plume	lure	fuse
plum	lunch	fuss
cute	tusk	cub
cut	tune	cube
mule	dune	rug
mud	dunk	rude

u words that end with **-e**

Fill in the missing letters.

Fill in **e** or **s.**

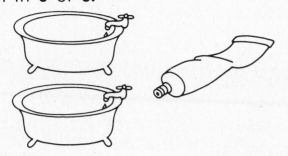

tub ___   tub ___

Fill in **e** or **s.**

cub ___   cub ___

Fill in **t** or **b.**

cu ___ e   cu ___ e

Fill in **e** or **p.**

plum ___   plum ___

Fill in **e** or **k.**

Jun ___   jun ___

Fill in **n** or **b.**

   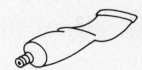

tu ___ e   tu ___ e

Fill in **e** or **s.**

fus ___   fus ___

Fill in **e** or **p.**

dun ___   dum ___

u words that end with -e

Fill in the blanks with the word part you need.

Fill in with –ube or –ub.

1. Mike left the toothpaste t_____ in the batht_____ .

2. The man carved two c_____s out of that one c_____ of wood.

Fill in with –ute or –ut.

1. I c_____ out four c_____ kittens from my coloring book.

2. He can act like a br_____, b_____ he is shy, too.

Fill in with –ule or –ug.

1. Mom has a r_____ about no wet feet on the r_____ .

2. Dad has a coffee m_____ with a picture of a m_____ on it.

Fill in with –ume or –um.

1. Her hat had one pl_____ that was the color of a pl_____ .

Fill in with –use or –uss.

1. Dad made a big f_____ when the f_____ went out.

Fill in with –use or –us.

1. Are those plates for _____ to _____ , too?

One thing or more than one?

Fill in the blanks to make the words match the pictures.

___ mule   ___ mule___

___ tube   ___ tube___

___ prune   ___ prune___

___ flute   ___ flute___

Read and add **-s** if you need it.

eight brown mule ___   He can play nine tune___.

the month of June ___   He is never rude___.

one box of small cube ___   The vet has a cure___.

four blue plume ___   She eats some prune___.

one rubber tube ___   She played the flute___.

a list of twelve rule___   Kittens are cute___.

Box in that part of each word that means <u>one</u> thing.

prunes	tusks	tubes	skunks
rules	flutes	trunks	cubes
tunes	gulps	plumes	mules

u words that end with -e

Circle the correct word for the picture in each box. You can box in the base word if you need to. Remember: If a word ends with **-e,** keep **e** with the base part.

tunes tucks	prunes prints	plumes plums
mules mills	flutes flaps	cures cuts
cubes cubs	dunes dusts	tubes tubs
dunes dumps	rules rusts	fuses fusses
floats flutes	mules malls	fumes foams

u words that end with **-e**

Print the correct word below each picture.

cube	plumes	flute	mule	tubes	rules
cubes	flutes	plume	tube	mules	rule

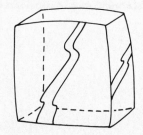

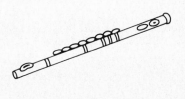

_____

IN CASE OF FIRE:
1. WALK
2. STAY IN LINE
3. NO TALKING

_____

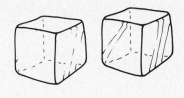

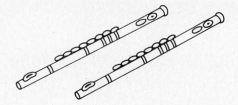

_____

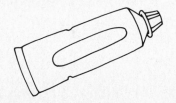

NO TALKING

_____

Adding endings to words that end with -e

Remember: When you want to add **-ed** or **-er** endings to words that end with **-e,** leave out one of the **e**'s.

Add **ed** to <u>cure</u> to get __ __ __ __ __.

Add **s** to <u>cure</u> to get __ __ __ __ __.

1. Our vet _____ our dog when he became ill.

2. A vet may use pills when he _____ sick dogs or cats.

Add **s** to <u>tune</u> to get __ __ __ __ __.

Add **ed** to <u>tune</u> to get __ __ __ __ __.

1. I can play some _____ on my trumpet.

2. The band _____ up before they played that song.

Add **er** to <u>rule</u> to get __ __ __ __ __.

Add **s** to <u>rule</u> to get __ __ __ __ __.

Add **ed** to <u>rule</u> to get __ __ __ __ __.

1. King James is the _____ of the land. Sometimes a queen may be ruler.

2. He has made some strict _____ from his throne.

3. Some kings and queens have _____ for a long time.

Add **-ed** or **-er.**

1. They use____ up the toothpaste.

2. He gulp____ down one milkshake.

3. This water is pure____ than that.

4. Dad prune____ four bushes.

5. An owl is a good hunt____.

6. She tune____ the harp.

Adding endings to words that end with -e

Remember: When you want to add **-ed** or **-er** endings to words that end with **-e,** leave out one of the **e**'s.

Add endings to the base words to make words with other meanings.

A teacher makes rule____ for the classroom.

We use a rule____ to help us make lines.

For the last five years the king rule____ the land alone.

The word <u>prune</u> can mean two things.

Prune____ can be a food that we eat.

If we have trimmed bushes or trees, we say that we

have prune____ them.

Each day Mom use____ pots and pans when she makes dinner.

When she cooks fish, she use____ a big skillet.

Last Sunday she use____ a big pot to cook corn on the cob.

Jane and Kate see a lot of cute stuffed rabbits at the store.

Kate thinks the blue one is cute____ than the white one.

Jane thinks the yellow rabbit is cute____ than the blue one.

Long ago men wore hats with plume____ .

Sometimes the colored plume____ came from peacocks.

The men of that time looked handsome in plume____ hats.

u words that end with **-e**

Box in the base word. Print the letters of the base word on the lines.

1. We get [mule]s from m u l e .

2. We get r u l e r from __ __ __ __ .

3. We get c u r e d from __ __ __ __ .

4. We get c u t e r from __ __ __ __ .

5. We get p l u m e s from __ __ __ __ __ .

6. We get u s e s from __ __ __ .

7. We get t u n e d from __ __ __ __ .

8. We get p u r e r from __ __ __ __ .

9. We get f u s e s from __ __ __ __ .

10. We get u s e d from __ __ __ .

Fill in the word that belongs. Use the words from the bottom of the page.

1. You can play sweet sounding tunes on it. _____

2. It is a square block with six sides. _____

3. It can be used to draw lines. _____

4. When fresh it is a plum; when dry it is a _____.

5. It is the name of a summer month. _____

6. Hills of sand along a lake or seashore are called _____.

7. Water that is clean and safe to drink is _____.

8. It has long ears and looks a little like a horse. _____

June   dunes   cube   pure   mule   ruler   prune   flute

u words that end with **-e**

Read these words. Do they all <u>end</u> with **-e**? _____ Do all but one have the vowel **u** in the <u>middle</u>? _____ Write the word that <u>begins</u> with **u.** _____

rule	cute	fuse	cube	tube	plume	use

Box in the base words.
If a word ends with **-e,** keep **e** with the base word.

Keep **e** with the base word		Keep **e** with the ending	
cuter	used	puffed	punted
tubes	ruler	brushed	stuffed
ruled	uses	fusses	ducked
fuses	plumes	munched	pulled
cubed	cubes	dumped	clucked

Circle the word that belongs in the sentence.

1. My yellow stuffed dog is (cuter, cutter, cubed) than my red one.

2. I got two (tugs, tubs, tubes) of toothpaste at the drugstore.

3. Kate loves to eat purple (plums, plumes, plumps) as a snack.

4. I am done cutting the (cubs, cubes, clubs) of cheese.

5. The little (cubs, clubs, cubes) played together in the den.

6. My little brother (fusses, fuses, fills) before his bedtime.

7. Dad went to the hardware store to get (fumes, buses, fuses).

8. He (under, used, until) five colors of paint for this picture.

9. Tell Joan the (ruler, ruled, rules) so that she can play, too.

Two ways to write the same sound

Write the words that have vowels that sound like the **u** or the **oo** in

pr $\boxed{u}$ n $\boxed{e}$ t $\boxed{oo}$ th

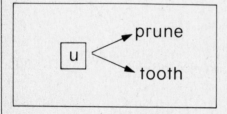

brushed	puzzle	1. _____
lure	tube	2. _____
scrubbed	buckle	3. _____
pure	clump	4. _____
scooter	groom	5. _____
shrubs	fume	6. _____
plume	grumble	7. _____
broom	use	8. _____
		9. _____

To get the base word in these words,
take off the ending and put the **e** back on.

-ed

used is ___use___ + _ed_

ruled is _____ + ____

tuned is _____ + ____

-er

ruler is ___rule___ + _er_

tuner is _____ + ____

user is _____ + ____

u words that end with -e

Read the sentence. Write the missing word on the line.

1. She took the _____ down from the shelf for a snack.
   prunes proms

2. We watched the _____ yellow chicks hatch out of the eggs.
   cute cut

3. Craig left the cap off the _____ of toothpaste again.
   tub tube

4. I filled four plates of oranges and _____ for snacks.
   plumes plums

5. He gives Jim a ride to _____ Scout meetings on Sundays.
   cube Cub

6. _____ broke two spokes on the wheel of her bike.
   June Junk

7. It was _____ when they pushed in front of the man.
   rude rub

8. We _____ eight pipe cleaners in arts and crafts class.
   cut cute

9. Miss Jones will _____ a globe when she teaches.
   use us

10. _____ and I are acting the parts of whales in the play.
    Luke Luck

11. Al hopes that he can take _____ lessons with me again.
    flunk flute

12. Whenever she sits in the _____ , she wants the rubber duck.
    tub tube

© 1995 SRA/McGraw-Hill

e words that end with -e

When you see **e**, you say the sound you hear in <u>red</u> and <u>ten</u>. Another sound for **e** is the sound you hear in <u>me</u> and <u>three</u>. Look at the pictures. Read the word you see in the box with the picture. Use the **e** sound that you hear in <u>me</u>. Do not say the **e** at the end of the words.

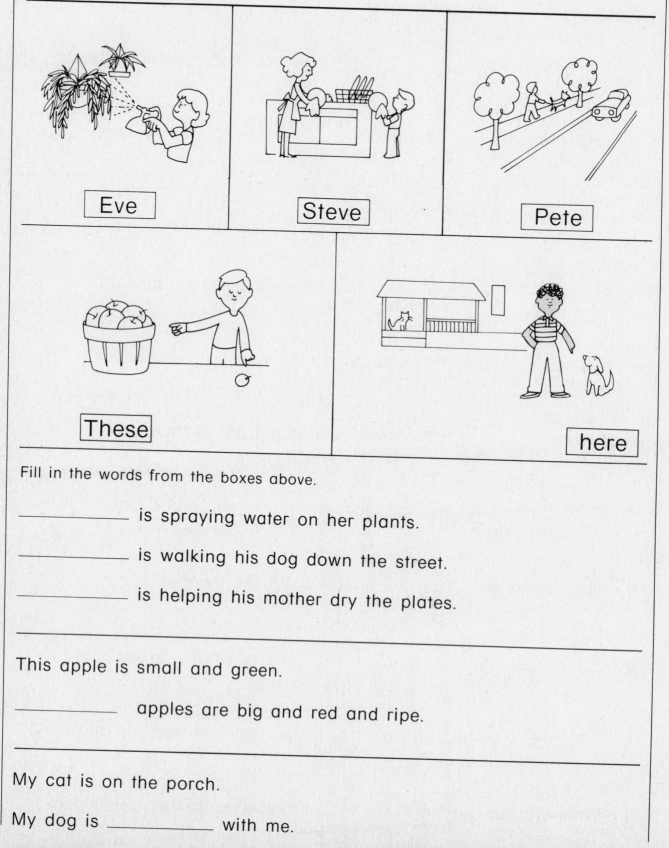

Eve

Steve

Pete

These

here

Fill in the words from the boxes above.

_____ is spraying water on her plants.

_____ is walking his dog down the street.

_____ is helping his mother dry the plates.

This apple is small and green.

_____ apples are big and red and ripe.

My cat is on the porch.

My dog is _____ with me.

Four ways to write the same sound

Write the words that have vowels that sound like **e** in

m [ea] t   gr [ee] n   b [e]   h [e] r [e]

she	shred	1. _____
queen	three	2. _____
freckle	melt	3. _____
press	these	4. _____
sneak	fleas	5. _____
Pete	held	6. _____
pebble	Steve	7. _____
me	wept	8. _____
		9. _____

Box in the base word.

weeping	queens	melts	screened
trees	helper	fleas	melting
melted	cleaning	rested	sneaks
heater	sneaking	cleaned	cleaner

e words that end with -e

Read the sentence. Write the missing word on the line.

1. When they sit down, the waiter will give _____ some buns.
   them   theme

2. Miss Twain says one rule in _____ class is no talking while
   here   her
   we read.

3. _____ asked if the gloves will shrink in hot water.
   Eve   Ever

4. The clerk says _____ four blue belts are the last ones left.
   this   these

5. Our _____ cat watched the two bees from the porch window.
   Pete   pet

6. Ask _____ to get your kite out of the bushes.
   stem   Steve

7. Did you _____ ride across town on the Main Street bus?
   Eve   ever

8. _____ saved five dollars and eight dimes in his bank.
   Pete   Pet

9. Go get the yellow quilt and bring it _____ so I can fix it.
   her   here

10. _____ spring we will plant gardens in our backyards.
    This   These

11. The white roses that Father gave Mother had long _____.
    Steves   stems

12. Luke brings trucks along so we can play with _____.
    them   theme

o, u, and e words that end with -e

Read the words beside the picture. Connect the correct word to the picture.

dune dome bean	real role rule	mule mole meal
probe preach prune	core keen cure	stove Steve stoop
Eve use one	tone team tune	flute fleet float
foam fear fume	here home dune	theme those soothe
rode rude read	June Jean Joan	tease tote tube

o, u, and e words that end with -e

Look at the picture. Read the words at the bottom of the page.
Circle each word that tells about something in the picture.

shovel	bone	stones	hole
rope	mule	smoke	Steve
prune	tube	cure	cone
roses	home	hose	tune
cube	fuse	rule	theme
shore	plume	rude	dune

a, i, o, u, and e words that end with -e

Read the words beside the picture. Connect the correct word to the picture.

mule / male	pole / pile	cure / core
ripe / rope	grove / grapes	rude / rode
here / hare	cone / cane	fumes / fines
Steve / stove	chase / chose	cute / gate
tire / tore	dome / dime	lake / like

a, i, o, u, and e words that end with -e

Read the words. Connect the correct words to the pictures.

ray		trike		pea	
raid		trip		Pete	
rake		try		pet	
rag		tribe		peel	

shin		wag		rod	
shine		way		robe	
shy		wave		road	
ship		wait		rope	

heel		pane		crime	
here		paid		crisp	
her		pad		cry	
heat		pay		crib	

plain		cub		stem	
plan		cute		steam	
play		cube		Steve	
plate		cut		steel	

sly		soap		bay	
slide		sole		bag	
slid		soak		bake	
slip		sock		bait	

a, i, o, u, and **e** words that end with **-e**

Circle the word you need to finish the sentence.

1.	You get toothpaste from a	hose	glass	jar	tube
2.	The opposite of <u>real</u> is	good	fake	belong	alone
3.	The month after May is	year	June	March	Sunday
4.	The opposite of <u>fresh</u> is	oven	dry	alive	stale
5.	If you win, you may get a	book	glove	prize	alarm
6.	To walk in water is to	dive	swim	splash	wade
7.	You put flowers into a	river	stove	vase	cover
8.	Digging leaves a	wood	shovel	hole	puddle
9.	One more than eight is	two	seven	nine	four
10.	The opposite of <u>save</u> is	bank	keep	loan	spend
11.	<u>Smart</u> means the same as	wise	good	think	teacher
12.	A man shaves to get rid of	wool	blades	skin	whiskers
13.	The opposite of <u>smile</u> is	grin	frown	wink	giggle
14.	Four sides make a	line	box	room	square
15.	<u>Slope</u> means to	hill	drift	fall	slant
16.	The opposite of <u>common</u> is	rare	none	often	away
17.	To be <u>scared</u> is to be	glad	tired	afraid	scream
18.	The opposite of <u>close</u> is	lift	near	by	far
19.	If you have none, you have	8	0	2	4
20.	The opposite of <u>above</u> is	on	beside	next to	beneath

a, i, o, u, and e words that end with -e

Read the riddle. Write the correct word on the blank line.
Use words from the bottom of the page.

This is in your kitchen.

It has an oven.

You bake and cook with it.

It is a _____.

This is a tool.

It may have a wooden handle.

You use it to gather leaves.

It is a _____.

This is used in yards.

It is long, thin, and round.

It is made of rubber.

Water sprays out of it.

It is a _____.

These are hard.

Dogs like them.

They are left when you are
    done eating spareribs.

They are _____.

This tastes sweet.

You may have it for dessert.

It has frosting on top and
    between the layers.

It is a _____.

It is flat and round.

You eat meals off it.

A fork and spoon may be
    next to it.

It is a _____.

It has thorns on its stem.

It can live in a garden.

It has buds before it blooms.

It smells good.

It is a _____.

Small children ride on it.

It has three wheels.

One wheel is in front.

Two wheels are in the back.

It is a _____.

---

ribbon	hose	scooter	trike	cake
shovel	stove	toaster	rose	pineapple
tree	plate	rake	shrub	bones

a, i, o, u, and **e** words that end with **-e**

Choose the word you need to finish the sentence. Write it on the line.

1. The thing that helps you walk is a _____ .
   cane   can

2. The things that are like hats are _____ .
   capes   caps

3. The things that fly in the air are _____ .
   skits   kites

4. We can wash and wax the _____ .
   tile   till

5. The clerk at the hardware store sells _____ and brooms.
   mops   mopes

6. The little rabbit _____ under the bushes.
   hops   hopes

7. We can see small _____ at the zoo.
   cubes   cubs

8. Will you tell _____ that I am here?
   theme   them

9. He will beat these eggs before he adds them to the _____
   cake   coke
   batter.

10. Miss Crane says we will plant bean sprouts again in _____ .
    Jane   June

11. Luke is glad he can come with us to lunch this _____ .
    time   tame

12. Eve and Pete had a good time picking up pine cones down
    by the _____ .
    late   lake

a, i, o, u, and **e** words that end with **-e**

Read the sentence. Write the missing word on the line.

1. The man in the flower shop put the orange _____
   beside the pot of ferns.   vases   vises

2. Pete will put butter in the frying pan that is on the _____ .
                                                stove   Steve

3. I need you to teach me the _____ so that we can play.
                              roles   rules

4. Gail held the gate as we pushed our _____ into the yard.
                                        bakes   bikes

5. Father pressed down on the _____ to stop the car.
                              brake   broke

6. _____ will smile if I tell those good jokes in school today.
   Stove   Steve

7. Liz and Jill wanted to take a boat _____ on the river.
                                        rode   ride

8. It is _____ not to say "thank you" when someone gives you
          rude   rode
   a gift.

9. All of us helped Dad to pull the sailboat up on _____ .
                                                    shore   share

10. My little sister sometimes forgets that she must _____
    when we are in the store.   behave   belong

11. Ann fixed the flat _____ on her bike.
                        time   tire

12. Jane is saving _____ so she can get baseball cards.
                    dimes   domes

Pattern words with -ie, -oe, -ue

Look at the words in the boxes and in the list below. Do these words all end with **e**? _____ Is the **e** next to a vowel in each of the words? _____ In words like these you say the letter name for **i, o,** and **u.** Read the words and the sentences in the boxes.

toe	pie	blue

This is a toe .

She is eating some pie .

He is coloring the sky blue .

Draw a line to match the correct word to the picture.

glue   pie

Joe   clue

blue   tie

doe   hoe

Choose the word you need from the list in the middle of the page. Print the missing consonants of the word in the blanks.

1. Dad uses a shovel and a _____oe in the garden.

2. Eve baked an apple _____ie for supper.

3. Steve put on his blue and white striped _____ie.

4. Jeff fixes his broken airplanes with _____ue.

5. Walter colored the water _____ue.

6. _____oe is all done cleaning his room.

7. A mother deer is called a _____oe.

8. We have no _____ue how our lost dog found his way home.

Pattern words with –ie, –oe, –ue

Choose the word you need to finish the sentence. Write it on the line.

pine   pie   pile   pin   pick

1. Pete wants some peach _____.
2. What book will you _____?
3. We raked the leaves into a _____.

hoe   hot   hose   home   hole

1. It is time for us to go _____.
2. Ann watered the garden with a _____.
3. Dad is digging up the garden with a _____.

cube   cute   clue   cub   cure

1. A little kitten is _____.
2. A square block is called a _____.
3. The spy is looking for a _____.

tire   time   tick   tie   tile

1. Mom needs soap and water to scrub the _____.
2. A clock tells _____.
3. Tom puts on a _____ before we go out to dinner.

true   tube   tune   tub   try

1. Luke will get his trumpet and play a _____.
2. Do not lie, but tell me something that is _____.
3. Glue sometimes comes in a _____.

Pattern words with **-ie, -oe, -ue**

Choose the word you need to finish the sentence. Write it on the line.

1. Sue and I will quit playing when dinner is _____.	do
2. The little deer was staying near the _____.	done
3. When are you going to _____ the dishes?	doe

1. The flowers in the vase will wilt and _____.	die
2. Eve is cutting that big _____ pickle in half.	dill
3. Here is a _____ to pay for these gumdrops.	dime

1. In the spring and summer our roses _____.	blue
2. I like the color _____ best of all.	bloom
3. **The farmer has a herd of white and _____ cows.**	black

1. Mom pulled the _____ of weeds from the garden.	club
2. The twins came to our _____ meeting Tuesday.	clue
3. The fingerprints will give us a _____ in this case.	clump

1. _____ is looking at a purple flowered dress.	use
2. **The Cub Scouts will _____ the campground today.**	Sue
3. Joe splashed _____ when he dove into the lake.	us

1. At _____ we will play outside before it gets dark.	hoe
2. Dad will dig some deep _____ to plant shrubs.	holes
3. You have to be strong to use that big _____.	home

ow as in snow

When you see **ow,** you say the sound you hear in <u>cow</u> and <u>brown</u>.

Another sound for **ow** is the sound you hear in 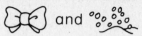 and .

Draw a line from the pictures that have the **ow** sound in <u>snow</u> to the letters in the middle of the page.

_OW_

ow as in snow

Look at the picture. Say the word. Fill in the missing letters.
Look at the sample to see how to do it.

bl ow

___ ow

___ ___ ow

___ ow

___ ow

___ ___ ___ ow

___ ow

___ ow ___

___ ___ ow

___ ow ___

___ ___ ow

___ ___ ow

___ ow

___ ow

ow as in snow

Read the words beside the pictures. Connect each word to the correct picture.

blow	growl	mow
bow	grow	moo
blouse	show	roar
blow	shore	row
book	crow	snow
bowl	crowd	snore
sow	boot	bow
soap	bowl	bowl

ow as in snow

Look at the picture. Say the word that names the picture. Choose the letter pair you need to finish the word. Write it on the line.

c ___ n ow or	sl ___ ou ow	h ___ k ow oo
m ___ oo ow	cr ___ ow oo	t ___ ch ow or
gl ___ or ow	st ___ l oo ow	fl ___ or ow
b ___ k oo ow	thr ___ ow or	st ___ k or ow
l ___ ow ou	sp ___ l ow oo	sh ___ ou ow

Two sounds of **ow**

Write the words below in the correct list.

| show | down | drown | low | slow | owl |
| crowd | how | blow | growl | grow | snow |

ow → bowl

ow → cow

_____   _____

_____   _____

_____   _____

_____   _____

_____   _____

Use the words below to fill in the correct word in each sentence.

| show | grow | flow | crow | tow |
| shower | growl | flower | crowd | town |

1. We live in a small _____ in Maine.

2. The small black _____ will die if its mother leaves.

3. Use a hoe to loosen the ground in the _____ garden.

4. My little sister gets afraid when she hears a dog _____.

5. Dad cannot start the car, so he is calling for a _____ truck.

6. All of us are going to the _____ together this afternoon.

7. A _____ gathered as they fed the seals at the zoo.

8. These two small plants will _____ to be four feet tall.

9. We stood and watched the river _____ around the rocks.

10. After a short rain _____, the sun made a rainbow.

Longer words with **ow**

Connect the words with the correct pictures.

pillow

hollow

rainbow

willow

below

follow

Read the sentence. Use the words below to fill in the blanks.

shallow   rainbow   willow   yellow   follow

window   swallow   hollow   borrow

1. Mom tells us to _____ our food before we talk.

2. The river was too _____ to swim in so we went home.

3. The branches of _____ trees have long, slender leaves.

4. My dog likes to _____ me whenever I go outside.

5. The barn owl likes to make its nest in _____ trees.

6. After the rain shower the sun made a _____ in the sky.

7. Our cat often sleeps on the _____ sill.

8. May I _____ your _____ scarf today?

Connect the words with the correct pictures.

snow blower

slower

bowler

owner

lower

mower

Choose the word you need to finish the sentence. Write it on the line.

1. The roots of a plant grow _____ the ground.
    below   belong

2. Mom will _____ my closet shelf so I can reach it.
    louder   lower

3. Do you think the _____ of that boat will let us borrow it?
    owner   our

4. The farmer has a rooster that _____ when the sun rises.
    crows   crowds

5. Cliff was a _____ skater than the rest, so he lost.
    sour   slower

6. I _____ two packs of gum.
    owe   ouch

7. Mother has a yellow quilt and a soft _____ for your bed.
    pulled   pillow

8. Sue added three cups of _____ to the pie crust.
    flour   flow

who, whose, where, there

Look at the picture. Read the question below the picture. Look at the next picture. Fill in the word you need to finish the sentence. In the rows below the pictures, circle all the words that are like the sample word.

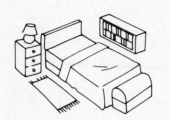 

| Where | is the pillow? | The pillow is under the _____. |

| where | which | here | where | there | where | were | wheel |

| Who | is pushing the cart? | Mother is pushing the _____. |

| who | how | who | where | how | why | way | who |

| There | is a line of children. | They will _____ in | there |. |

| there | the | where | they | here | there | there | then |

| Whose | bottle of glue is this? | It is _____ bottle of glue. |

| whose | who | where | how | whose | why | show | whose |

who, whose, where, there

Use one of the words below to fill in the word that belongs in the blank.
Write it on the line.

who   whose   where   there

1. Is someone in the kitchen?

   _____ is in the kitchen?

2. Are the children going somewhere today?

   _____ are all these children going?

3. Is someone in the boat?

   Let us see _____ is in the boat.

4. Here is a cute gray and white kitten.

   _____ kitten is it?

5. Are there some crackers left?

   _____ are no more crackers on the plate.

6. Did someone see the baseball?

   _____ did the baseball go?

7. Here is a good pair of gloves.

   _____ gloves are these?

8. Is there something we can do to fix the tile?

   _____ is a wide scratch in the tile.

who, whose, where, there

Read the question. Circle the correct word.

1. Where do geese fly before winter? ....south   north   west

2. Who counts the cash? ....dime   bother   clerk

3. Where do sharks and whales live? ....sea   lake   say

4. Who can have a snout? ....pig   goose   bird

5. What is filled with toothpaste? ....jar   tube   tape

6. When do flowers grow? ....yard   spring   supper

7. Who growls at a prowler? ....match   dog   crook

8. Where do we use a hoe? ....fall   garden   yelp

9. Who makes you smile? ....crown   joke   clown

10. When do apples ripen? ....winter   fall   pie

11. Where do we get coal from? ....mine   grill   fire

12. Where do we use some hangers? .....close   wire   closet

13. Who grades our quizzes? ....school   test   teacher

14. Where can you look at a chimp? .....farm   room   zoo

15. Where can a rocket fly? ....moon   noon   blast

16. Where do cows and horses belong? ..house   milk   barn

17. Whose nest is in a hollow tree? ......owl   owner   mule

18. Whose job is it to grow food? ....farmer   beans   morning

19. Who plays football? ....theme   team   there

20. What keeps your hands warm? ......glue   growl   gloves

21. Who reads books? ....kitten   children   yellow

22. What is a name of a tree? ....watch   plate   willow

Review

Look at the picture. Read the words below the picture. Circle each word that tells about something in the picture.

shovel	foot	water	trike	beach	tire
book	rainbow	hood	plate	glue	show
pie	rope	prune	bowl	grapes	stripes
clue	crow	smoke	boat	gloves	benches
basket	oven	scraper	toe	pole	inner tube
pail	window	river	tie	pillow	swings

Review

Read the words and look at the picture. Make a good sentence from the words and write it on the line.

baked   Who

pies   those

apple   two

1. _____?

do   put

I   the

hoe   Where

2. _____?

ducks   eight

there   Are

3. _____?

Whose   are

gloves   these

4. _____?

vase   They

broken   glued

the

5. _____.

Contractions with will

When we talk we sometimes put two words together and they sound like one word. When we do this we leave out a sound from one of the words. In reading, we see a mark like ['] to show where a letter was left out. We call these words contractions.

Read the two words. Cross out the letters that will be left out.
Write and read the contraction. Look at the sample to see how to do it.

she will ——▶ she ~~wi~~ll ——▶ she'll

he will ——▶ he will ——▶ __ __ , __ __

we will ——▶ we will ——▶ __ __ , __ __

it will ——▶ it will ——▶ __ __ __ , __

I will ——▶ I will ——▶ __ __ , __

you will ——▶ you will ——▶ __ __ __ , __ __

they will ——▶ they will ——▶ __ __ __ __ , __ __

Read the sentence. Circle the contraction you need to finish the sentence.

1. (She'll, It'll) have to look for her book that is due.

2. (He'll, It'll) take me a long time to shovel the driveway.

3. (They'll, I'll) all be here between one and two o'clock.

Make these words into contractions. Use the contractions below.

you will ——▶ __ __ __ , __ __   we will ——▶ __ __ , __ __

it will ——▶ __ __ , __ __   I will ——▶ __ , __ __

we'll   I'll   you'll   it'll

Print the words these contractions are made of.

she'll ➞ s h e w i l l   it'll ➞ __ __ __ __ __ __

they'll ➞ __ __ __ __ __ __ __ __   he'll ➞ __ __ __ __ __ __

you'll ➞ __ __ __ __ __ __ __   we'll ➞ __ __ __ __ __ __

who'll ➞ __ __ __ __ __ __ __   I'll ➞ __ __ __ __ __

In the blank, write the two words the contraction is made of.

1. He says that _____ be done by twelve o'clock.
   he'll

2. Next month _____ be going on a four week trip.
   we'll

3. If you have glue, _____ fix this broken frame.
   I'll

4. _____ have to get film before you leave for camp.
   You'll

5. _____ bring the food for our lunch?
   Who'll

Look at the [,] in I'<u>ll</u>. Is it on the line? _____ Is it below the

line? _____ Is it above the line? _____ Now try to make some

yourself. Start with a round dot. Then hang a tail from the

top of the dot like this: [•][•][•,][,][,][,]

Now make some of your own. [•][•][•][ ][ ][ ]

Longer words with two <u>different</u> consonants in the middle

You remember that to help yourself read longer words with twin consonants in the middle, you split the word between the twin consonants. You do the same thing to read a longer word with two middle consonants that are <u>different</u>.

Split these words between the two middle consonants. Box in and read the two parts of the word. Print the letters on the lines.

| t r a c | t o r | is | trac tor |

infant   is _____

walrus   is _____

fifteen   is _____

dentist   is _____

helmet   is _____

shampoo   is _____

butler   is _____

organ   is _____

cobweb   is _____

Longer words with two <u>different</u> consonants in the middle

These words are split between the two middle consonants. Read the two parts.
Put the two parts together and print the word on the line. Read the word.

pret • zel   is _pretzel_____

chip • munk   is _____

<u>tar</u> • <u>get</u>   is _____

<u>bar</u> • <u>ber</u>   is _____

<u>pad</u> • <u>lock</u>   is _____

<u>cac</u> • <u>tus</u>   is _____

<u>ser</u> • vant   is _____

<u>nap</u> • <u>kin</u>   is _____

<u>lum</u> • <u>ber</u>   is _____

<u>car</u> • <u>toon</u>   is _____

Longer words with two <u>different</u> consonants in the middle

Split these words between the different middle consonants. Read the two parts and write the words below the right pictures.

magnet   picnic   mustard   person   number   costume

doctor   igloo   thermos   insect   lantern   tadpole

Longer words with two <u>different</u> consonants in the middle

Choose the word you need to finish the sentence. Write it on the line.

mistakes   perfect   forget

1. No one person is _____.

2. It is true that we all make _____.

canteens   compass   canvas

1. He'll use a _____ to show where he is going.

2. The scouts took _____ of water for the hike.

doctor   dentist   barber

1. Who helps you to get well when you are sick? _____

2. Who cuts your hair when it gets too long? _____

cactus   carpet   cartons

1. The big tall plant in our front room is a _____.

2. We like to use egg _____ to make things in art class.

organ   order   often

1. Do you have to water those rose bushes _____?

2. The bride had someone play the _____ at her wedding.

Longer words that end in **-y**

Sometimes **-y** at the end of a longer word sounds like **ee**. Read the sentences that tell about the pictures. <u>Hear</u> how **-y** at the end of a word sounds like **ee**.

The ⬚sun⬚ is out today.

It is a ⬚sunny⬚ day.

This is her ⬚dad⬚ .

She calls him ⬚Daddy⬚ .

Liz stepped in the ⬚mud⬚ .

Her feet are ⬚muddy⬚ .

This is his ⬚mom⬚ .

He calls her ⬚Mommy⬚ .

Read the words. Connect the words to the correct pictures.

jelly

kitty

grassy

shaggy

puppy

funny

Write the correct word in the blanks of the sentences.

messy   foggy   dizzy   hobby

1. If you spin around again and again, you'll get _____.

2. Pete needs a napkin to wipe his _____ hands.

3. Sometimes it can be _____ outside.

4. Dave collected baseball cards as his _____.

Longer words that end with -y

At the end of these words, the **-y** sounds like **ee.** Read the sentences that tell about the pictures. Fill in the blanks by adding **-y** to the word in the box.

That is a big | bump | .

This is a ⬚bumpy⬚ road.

A dark | cloud | covered the sky.

It was a _____ day.

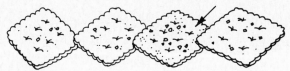

This cracker has | salt | on it.

It is a _____ cracker.

The glue will | stick | to your hands.

It is _____ glue.

Add **-ing** or **-y** to finish the sentences.

1. Mom is dust_____ the house.

    The house is dust_____ .

2. Look at how hard it is snow_____ .

    It is a snow_____ day.

3. That is stick_____ glue.

    The glue is stick_____ to his fingers.

4. I hear one of my bike wheels squeak_____ when I ride.

    My bike has a squeak_____ wheel.

5. Randy is crunch_____ on that pretzel.

    That pretzel is crunch_____ .

6. Joe felt sleep_____ all day long.

    Now he is sleep_____ on his bed.

Longer words that end with **-y**

Connect each word with the correct picture.

candy

daisy

starry

story

fairy

copy

Write in the word you need to finish the sentence.

1. Sue is drinking root beer with a lot of foam on it.

   It is a _____ drink.

2. The wind is blowing outside today.

   It is a _____ day.

3. This pipe is leaking water from a small hole.

   This is a _____ pipe.

4. Joe is playing in the sand on the beach.

   Joe is playing on the _____ beach.

5. When there is a storm, we have rain and thunder.

   Rain and thunder come on a _____ day.

6. The fender on that car is rusting.

   It is a _____ fender.

Longer words that end with **-y**

Write the correct word below each picture.

cloudy	starry	candy	fairy	grassy	leaky
daisy	rusty	frosty	poppy	sticky	copy

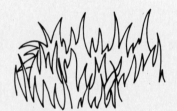

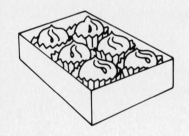

Longer words that end with -y

Use one of these words to finish each sentence.

---

copy   daisy   skinny   funny   jelly

candy   leaky   sleepy   soapy   easy

1. Some men are fat and some men are not fat.

   The opposite of fat is _____.

2. I picked a yellow and white flower that was growing in the yard.

   The flower was a _____ .

3. Gumdrops are sweet and taste good.

   Gumdrops are _____ .

4. Water comes into the boat when we try to take a ride.

   That is a _____ boat.

5. Wendy did not rinse that one glass well.

   That one glass is _____ .

6. Steve was awake for a long time.

   He is getting _____ .

7. I'll put some peanut butter on my sandwich.

   I like peanut butter with _____ .

8. Peggy will make a vase just like the teacher made.

   She'll _____ the vase that the teacher made.

9. Some things are not hard to do.

   These things are _____ to do.

10. Rich watched two cartoons on Sunday morning.

    Good cartoons can be _____ .

Longer words that end with -ly

At the end of a longer word, the **-ly** sounds like **lee.** Read the sentences that tell about the pictures. Fill in the blanks by adding **-ly** to the unfinished word in each picture box.

She is quick about cleaning.

She cleans quick_____.

That is a slow horse.

That horse trots slow_____.

That dog has a loud bark.

That dog is barking loud_____.

Mom is a safe driver.

She drives safe_____.

Fill in the correct word to finish the sentence.

clearly   lonely   daily   bravely   softly

sadly   safely   ugly   weekly

1. Sandy will not talk loudly. She'll talk _____.

2. Tim is not happy saying good-bye. He says

   good-bye _____.

3. Andy brushes his teeth each day. He brushes his

   teeth _____.

4. The puppy is all alone. The puppy is _____.

5. The opposite of <u>pretty</u> is _____.

6. Look two ways before crossing the street and you will

   cross _____.

7. My brother washes his car each week. He washes his

   car _____.

8. Peg can see the chalkboard well. She sees it _____.

9. Richy is not afraid to do it. He'll do it _____.

any, many, very, every

Try to remember how these words look and sound.
Fill in the blanks. Use the words from the side.

1. We ate all the popcorn. We do not have _____ left.   every

2. All the children did not go, but _____ of them did.   any

3. We read and study math _____ day at school.   many

4. Did you _____ see a dog as handsome as this one?   very

5. We came home _____ tired after our long hike.   ever

Circle all the words that match the sample word at the left side.

many	any	many	nanny	many	may	man	many
every	every	very	every	ever	every	never	very
any	Andy	any	any	many	and	any	may
very	ever	every	very	never	very	ever	very

Read the questions. Circle yes or no.

1. Is it good to brush your teeth every day?   yes   no

2. Do any children like to eat liver?   yes   no

3. Do very many children like to eat liver?   yes   no

Fill in the blanks with any or every to make longer words.

1. I have looked _____where for my notebook.

2. I cannot see my notebook _____where.

3. He did not want _____thing to eat or drink.

4. My little sister wants to go _____where with me.

5. Can _____one tell me what to do next?

6. I think _____one will be there at the show.

Longer words that end with -y, -ly, -ty

Circle <u>yes</u> or <u>no</u> if you think the sentence is true or not.

1. If someone is wide awake, that person is sleepy........yes   no

2. When it is foggy outside, you can see things clearly....yes   no

3. Cartoons and jokes are funny. ....yes   no

4. When many dark clouds are in the sky, it is likely
   to rain. ....yes   no

5. An apple pie can be freshly baked. ....yes   no

6. If your printing is done neatly, it is messy.............yes   no

7. When it snows hard all day, there is plenty of snow. ...yes   no

8. If you paid very little for a used car, you got it
   cheaply. ....yes   no

9. We can have fun and play games at a party. ....yes   no

10. A little puppy can have shaggy hair...................yes   no

11. If you have hardly any cash, you have plenty of cash..yes   no

12. If someone says something sweetly, that person is
    saying it nasty. ....yes   no

13. The sky can sometimes be starry......................yes   no

14. The car will drive smoothly on the bumpy road........yes   no

15. A cactus can be thorny and prickly. ....yes   no

16. We can swim safely where the water is shallow. ....yes   no

17. Children who run and play all day get sleepy. ....yes   no

18. Many children can belong to a club...................yes   no

19. Thinking of safety at home and in the street is wise....yes   no

20. The teacher can read the short book quickly. ....yes   no

Longer words that end with -y, -ly, -ty

Connect the words and the numbers.

20	fifty	60	eighty
40	twenty	80	seventy
50	forty	70	sixty

Read the questions. Circle the correct word.

1. Do quilts have any stuffing? ....yes   no

2. How many toes do two feet have? ....ten   five

3. How many covers are on a book? ....twelve   two

4. Is seventeen more than seventy? ....yes   no

5. Can a book have many chapters? ....yes   no

6. Can a man ever be forty? ....yes   no

7. Are there any apples in an apple pie? ....yes   no

8. Do insects have any elbows? ....yes   no

9. Can a spy use many clues? ....yes   no

10. Do rivers have any fish? ....yes   no

11. How many numbers are there on a clock? ....two   twelve

12. How many fingers are there on one glove?........five   ten

13. Are there any bones in a peach? ....yes   no

14. Are there any tires on a kite?......................yes   no

15. Are there fifty seats on a tractor?..................yes   no

Contractions with <u>not</u>

Read the two words. Cross out the letter that will be left out. Write and read the contraction.

Look at the samples. The star ★ tells you that the contraction for <u>cannot</u> is different from the others. Can you tell how?

did not ⟶ did no~~t~~ ⟶ **d i d n ' t**

★ cannot ⟶ can ~~not~~ ⟶ **c a n ' t**

are not ⟶ are not ⟶ _ _ _ _ _ ,

is not ⟶ is not ⟶ _ _ _ _ ,

has not ⟶ has not ⟶ _ _ _ _ _ ,

had not ⟶ had not ⟶ _ _ _ _ _ ,

was not ⟶ was not ⟶ _ _ _ _ _ ,

must not ⟶ must not ⟶ _ _ _ _ _ _ ,

have not ⟶ have not ⟶ _ _ _ _ _ _

Read the sentence. Circle the contraction you need.

1. Dad says we (haven't, can't) have any more pie to eat.

2. Vicky (didn't, hadn't) want to share her candy with anyone.

3. There (hadn't, aren't) very many kids here at the party yet.

Make these words into contractions. Use the contractions below.

was not ⟶ _ _ _ _ _ ,   has not ⟶ _ _ _ _ _ ,

had not ⟶ _ _ _ _ _ ,   is not ⟶ _ _ _ _ ,

hasn't   wasn't   hadn't   isn't

Contractions with <u>not</u>

Print the words these contractions are made of.

hasn't → __ __ __ __ __ __   haven't → __ __ __ __ __ __ __

wasn't → __ __ __ __ __ __   mustn't → __ __ __ __ __ __ __

aren't → __ __ __ __ __ __   hadn't → __ __ __ __ __ __

can't → __ __ __ __ __ __   didn't → __ __ __ __ __ __

In the blank, write the two words the contraction is made of.

1. Betsy _____ going to enter the art contest.
           wasn't

2. She _____ forget to take the note to the teacher.
         mustn't

3. Which classmates _____ come to the party?
                      can't

4. I _____ solved all the crossword puzzles yet.
       haven't

Write the words as contractions.

was not → __ __ __ __ __   did not → __ __ __ __ __
              '   '

is not → __ __ __ __   are not → __ __ __ __ __
             '   '

must not → __ __ __ __ __ __   had not → __ __ __ __ __
               '   '

Write the contraction in the blank.

1. We'll go where the beaches _____ so crowded.
                                are not

2. _____ the snapshot album somewhere by the bookshelves?
      Is not

3. Sue and Steve _____ want to go home yet.
                    did not

what, were, said

Read the short story below each picture. Use the words from the side of the page to write in the word you need. In the row just below the story, box in all the words that are like the sample word.

What	can you see on the counter? _____	cake
What	can you see in the skillet? _____	bowls
What	can you see in the oven? _____	pork chops

what	that	were	what	hat	when	what	was

The children | were | _____ to be at the zoo. | There
Goats and rabbits | were | _____ all around. | happy
_____ | were | many things to look at. | hopping

were	were	where	when	were	what	went

Mom | said | that she liked to _____ in this store. | wanted
Sandy | said | that she wanted a _____ dress. | striped
Pete | said | that he _____ that pair of gloves. | shop

said	said	sad	said	sob	said	sip	sail	said

what, were, said

1. Read the story. Fill in **what, were,** or **said.**
2. Read the question. Put an X on the correct blank line.

1.
Four children _____ going out for a day in the woods.

They had a blanket, a basket of food, a baseball, and a bat.

The children _____ looking for a spot to put down the

blanket and eat. One of them _____ that he wanted to sit

under the trees by the lake. _____ a good spot he found!

2.   What do you think they were going to do?

_____ watch a baseball game

_____ have a picnic

_____ play outside in the backyard

1.
Mom put the coffee pot on the stove and the muffins in the oven.

Dad came into the kitchen. He asked Mom for two eggs to cook.

Then Mom asked Dad _____ else he wanted with the eggs.

Dad _____ that all he wanted _____ the muffins and the

eggs. After they _____ done eating, Dad helped with the dishes.

2.   Where were Mom and Dad?

_____ by the kitten

_____ eating dinner

_____ in the kitchen

Review

Read the question and the words below it. Then circle the correct words.

What can you eat?

pineapple	swallow	prunes	napkin	cupcakes
pancake	pie	jelly	pretzel	grapes
cook	mustard	hoe	candy	plastic

Which of these are parts of your body?

bones	elbow	doctor	glue	nose
shampoo	finger	toe	spine	liver
foot	grow	ankle	tie	helmet

How can a person feel?

sleepy	windy	itchy	fluffy	grouchy
afraid	mad	happy	fussy	hollow
sick	silly	sad	glad	grumpy

What can be round?

dime	globe	tire	cake	pancake
pie	cube	stone	rainbow	ruler
bowl	baseball	book	plate	wastebasket

Where do you see snowflakes?

bathroom	winter	outside	inside	in the sky

Where can you swim?

fish tank	pool	puddle	lake	river

Where is a good picnic spot?

beach	park	chicken	woods	basket

Review

Look at the picture. Read the story and fill in the missing words.
Choose them from the bottom of the page.

Twenty Cub _____ spent a sunny weekend camping in the
woods. They took a compass, backpacks, and canteens with them.
When the bus got to the _____ ground, all the Scouts quickly
hopped out of the bus and _____ around. _____ of them
said that he found a perfect spot to pitch a _____. They
helped to take the things out of the _____ and get settled. Some
Scouts went down to the_____ with fishing poles and bait.
They wanted to see what the water was like. There were some
row _____ on the shore. The water was _____, so
they pushed two _____ in and got in themselves. On the bank,
they made a big _____ to fry _____.

fish	camp	river	shallow	boats	fire
boats	One	tent	Scouts	bus	looked

Review

This is a code.

$$\frac{a}{1} \quad \frac{e}{2} \quad \frac{i}{3} \quad \frac{o}{4} \quad \frac{u}{5} \quad \frac{y}{6}$$

Print the vowels on the blank lines to see what the sentence says.
Then circle the correct word or words below each sentence.

Wh__t d__ y__ __ s__ __ wh__n y__ __ l__ __v__?
  1   4   4 5   1 6   2   4 5   2 1 2

Thank you   Good-bye   Good morning

Th__s __s sp__n t__ tr__p __ns__cts.
 3   3   5   4   1   3 2

cobweb   insect   ant

W__ __ __t th__s w__th p__ __n__t b__tt__r.
 2   2 1   3   3   2 1 5   5 2

guppy   jelly   jumpy

Wh__r__ __r__ th__r__ m__n__ d__ __r?
 2 2   1 2   2 2   1 6   2 2

woods   webs   doe

Th__s __s __n the sk__ __nd h__s m__n__ c__l__rs.
 3   3   3   6   1   1   1 6   4 4

moon   sun   rainbow

Dr. Mr. Mrs.

Look at the pictures. Read the sentences.

This man is a doctor.
Call him Dr. Woods.

This is my father.
Call him Mr. Jones.

This is my mother.
Call her Mrs. Jones.

Fill in **Dr.** or **Mr.** or **Mrs.** You must use this mark [.] after each one.

1. The vet who gives our cat and dog shots is _____ Klopp.

2. The dentist who takes good care of our teeth is _____ Baxter.

3. The wife of Mr. Carter is _____ Carter.

4. The husband of Mrs. Baker is _____ Baker.

5. They call Joe Stevens, _____ Stevens.

6. My mother is _____ Morton.

7. My father is _____ Morton.

8. The doctor who gives us our yearly checkups is _____ Brown.

9. A man is called _____ .

10. A doctor is called _____ .

Read the sentences and write the word you need in the blank.

Dr. Miller took care of my little brother when he was sick.

Dr. Miller is a good _____ .
　　　　　　　　　doctor　dollar

Mr. Carson is our math teacher. Mr. Carson is a _____ .
　　　　　　　　　　　　　　　　　　　　man　mother

Mrs. Fisher has three children. Mrs. Fisher is a _____ .
　　　　　　　　　　　　　　　　　　　　man　mother

Adding -ing to words that end with -e

When **-ing** is added to a word that ends with **-e,** the **e** disappears!
You do not need **e** and **i** together in the ending.

Some of these words end with **-e** and some do not.
  1. Neatly circle the **e** in the base words.
  2. See what happens when you add **-ing.**

bake   +   ing ⟶ bak~~e~~ing ⟶ baking

crack   +   ing ⟶ cracking

wish   +   ing ⟶ wishing

strike   +   ing ⟶ strik~~e~~ing ⟶ striking

To add **-ing,** you leave out the **e** on the base word.
Read and write the base word together with the ending.

slid~~e~~ sliding   hope _____   shake_____

make _____   pile _____   use _____

smoke _____   chase _____   drive _____

tune _____   joke _____   rule _____

To get the base word, you take off **-ing** and put the **e** back on.

tak~~ing~~ is ___take___ + ___ing___   waking is _____ + _____

stroking is _____ + _____   driving is _____ + _____

hiding is _____ + _____   curing is _____ + _____

pruning is_____ + _____   closing is_____ + _____

Adding -ing to words that end with -e

1. Look for the **V**owel-**C**onsonant-**V**owel pattern.
2. Say "**V**owel-**C**onsonant-**V**owel" as you box in the pattern.
3. Say the first vowel name. Read the word.
4. Write the word on the line if it belongs in the Vowel Name Word List.

		Vowel Name Word List
w⎡ide⎤r	voting	wider _____
chasing	spotted	_____ _____
rubbed	gliding	_____ _____
tame	blaming	_____ _____
ruling	slip	_____ _____
packing	stroking	_____ _____
while	tuning	

Choose the correct word and write it in the blank. Box in the **V**owel-**C**onsonant-**V**owel pattern before you choose. Think of it as the **VCV** pattern.

1. Jane and Mike are _____ the dishes. (whipping, wiping)

2. The farmers are _____ it will rain. (hoping, hopping)

3. They are _____ the torn page together. (tapping, taping)

4. My big sister is _____ her nails. (filing, filling)

5. Dad is _____ paint off the window. (scraping, scrapping)

6. We are _____ our dog to the vet. (tacking, taking)

Remember how the **-e** disappears when **-ing** is added.
Circle the correct word and write it on the line.

_____

Dad will <u>make</u> a bookshelf.

Dad is (makeing, making) a bookshelf.   _____

We <u>hope</u> the sun will shine today.

We are (hopeing, hoping) it will not rain.   _____

She likes to <u>pile</u> blocks into a tower.

She is (piling, pileing) up the blocks.   _____

We will <u>use</u> the paints he gave us.

We are (useing, using) the paints we got.   _____

It is fun to <u>rake</u> leaves in the fall.

Everyone is (raking, rakeing) leaves.   _____

_____

Match the words. Draw a line to connect them.

make	marking
bake	backing
mark	making
back	baking
rake	rocking
rock	raking
wake	walking
walk	waking

Adding **-ing** to words that end with **-e**

When you see these words, you need to remember what the base word is.

Look for the base words in the rows below.
Write each one on the line where it belongs.

shaking _____   shining _____   choking _____

tuning _____   smoking _____   sliding _____

shin   smock   shine   shake   tuck   slide

smoke   tune   choke   slip   chop   shake

Add **-ing** to the base word below each line. Remember the disappearing **e**.
At the end of each sentence, write the word that belongs on the line.

1. Jeff is __taking__ his jacket to the __game__ .

take   gum   game

2. Ms. Wade is _____ the store at _____ .

close   sit   six

3. The cows are _____ on the _____ .

graze   grass   green

4. Our teacher is _____ our reading _____ .

time   texts   tests

5. I am _____ our puppy around the _____ .

chase   yarn   yard

6. The queen is _____ her _____ .

rule   land   loan

The disappearing **e**

Do you remember that when you add **-er, -ed,** or **-en** to words that end with **-e,** one of the **e**'s dissapears?

Circle the correct word. Remember: <u>One **e** must disappear!</u>

chase + ed is (chased, chaseed)

wipe + er is (wipeer, wiper)

spoke + en is (spoken, spokeen)

use + ed is (useed, used)

ripe + en is (ripeen, ripen)

vote + ed is (voted, voteed)

Add **-ed, -er,** or **-en** to the base word below the line.
At the end of the sentence, write the word that belongs on the line.

1. Mr. Good _____ the paint he got at the _____ .
   use   store   stone

2. My poodle was _____ the winner in the _____ .
   chose   shore   show

3. The _____ jumped off the diving _____ .
   dive   barked   board

4. The hang _____ floated to a smooth _____ .
   glide   landing   looking

Contractions with <u>is</u> and <u>have</u>

Read the two words. Cross out the letter or letters that will be left out.
Write and read the contractions. Look at the samples.

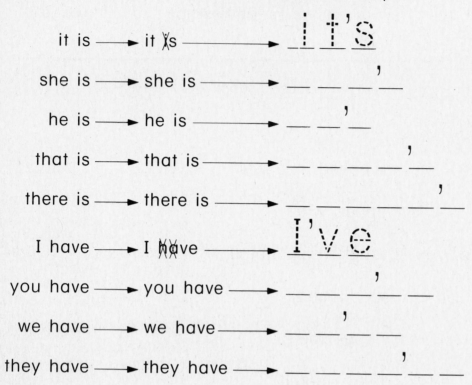

it is ——→ it i̶s ——→ _i t ' s_

she is ——→ she is ——→ __ __ __ ' __

he is ——→ he is ——→ __ __ ' __

that is ——→ that is ——→ __ __ __ __ ' __

there is ——→ there is ——→ __ __ __ __ __ ' __

I have ——→ I h̶a̶ve ——→ _I ' v e_

you have ——→ you have ——→ __ __ __ __ ' __

we have ——→ we have ——→ __ __ __ ' __

they have ——→ they have ——→ __ __ __ __ ' __ __

Read the sentence. Circle the contraction you need.

1. Who said (there's, he's) not much time before the show begins?

2. **That was the fastest speedboat (that's, we've) ever ridden in!**

3. (I've, It's) scraped my left elbow on that rusty gate.

4. He said (you've, that's) begun taking horseback riding lessons.

5. (There's, She's) not using the orange paint now.

6. Dr. Sherman said (he's, it's) time for your yearly checkup.

Make these words into contractions. Use the contractions below.

they have ——→ __ __ __ __ ' __   we have ——→ __ __ __ ' __

there is ——→ __ __ __ __ __ ' __   that is ——→ __ __ __ __ ' __

you have ——→ __ __ __ __ ' __   it is ——→ __ __ ' __

we've   you've   there's   it's   they've   that's

Contractions with is and have

Print the words these contractions are made of.

they've ➡ _ _ _ _ _ _ _ _   it's ➡ _ _ _ _

you've ➡ _ _ _ _ _ _ _   I've ➡ _ _ _ _ _

we've ➡ _ _ _ _ _ _   that's ➡ _ _ _ _ _ _

there's ➡ _ _ _ _ _ _ _ _   he's ➡ _ _ _ _ _

Write the two words the contraction is made of.

1. She said ___there is___ going to be a swimming party at the lake.
there's

2. They hope to win the contest _____ entered.
they've

3. Where do you think _____ going next weekend?
he's

4. _____ never finished the dishes so quickly before.
We've

Make the words into contractions. Write them on the lines.

that is ➡ _____   they have ➡ _____

we have ➡ _____   there is ➡ _____

you have ➡ _____   he is ➡ _____

Write the two words as a contraction to finish the sentence.

1. Mrs. Carter said that _____ time for us to go home now.
it is

2. Pete said _____ the best jelly he's ever tasted.
that is

3. Do you see what _____ making with those egg cartons?
he is

Pattern words with **-old, -olk, -oll, -olt, -ost**

These words all have the **o** sound in <u>go</u>, <u>boat</u>, <u>rose</u>, and <u>snow</u>.
Look at the pictures. Read the sentence that tells about the picture.

This ring is boxed{gold} .

A ball can boxed{roll} .

Here is a boxed{post} .

Connect the words to the correct picture.

old

colt

cold

toll

yolk

fold

most

scold

Choose the correct word. Write it in the blank.

roll   most   yolk   hold   colt   told

1. He will _____ onto the railing as he walks downstairs.

2. The small _____ was with his mother in the barn.

3. Cathy wants you to put butter on her dinner _____ .

4. Mom _____ me that we have to clean up now.

5. Bobby said that _____ of his math problems are done.

6. My little brother left the egg _____ on his plate.

Pattern words with -old, -olk, -oll, -olt, -ost

Choose one or two. Mark an X neatly on the blank line.

1. You put on a scarf, mittens, boots, and a hat when it is—

   _____ a very cold, snowy day.

   _____ a very hot, summer day.

   _____ a very windy, rainy, spring day.

2. What can you do with a ball?

   _____ Roll it across the yard.

   _____ Eat it on a dinner roll.

   _____ Toss it to the moon.

3. What is there inside an eggshell?

   _____ an egg yolk that is yellow

   _____ a peanut that is crunchy

   _____ egg white that is around the yolk

4. Where do you see the most plants?

   _____ in a yard covered with snow

   _____ on a small window sill

   _____ in a big garden in June

5. What can you see in a fish tank?

   _____ a little tadpole

   _____ some goldfish swimming

   _____ a real sailboat

Pattern words with -ild, -ind

These words all have the **i** sound in <u>I</u>, <u>ride</u>, and <u>pie</u>. Look at the pictures.
Read the sentences that tell about the picture.

The ape is not tame.
It is | wild | .

His pet dog is lost.
He'll | find | it.

She can't see.
She is | blind | .

He isn't grown up.
He is a | child | .

His clock stopped.
He'll have to | wind | it.

She's never mean to the cat.
She is | kind | .

Choose the correct word. Write it in the blank.

child   blind   hind   wind   mind   find

1. He'll have to _____ the yarn up into a ball.

2. A four-year-old is called a _____ .

3. Mrs. Kelly helped me _____ my lost jacket.

4. Do you think he'll _____ if we use his bike?

5. We need a _____ fold to play the game.

6. Dr. Porter put a cast on the _____ leg of my dog.

Pattern words with -ild, -ind

Do this crossword puzzle. Use the words from the bottom of the page.

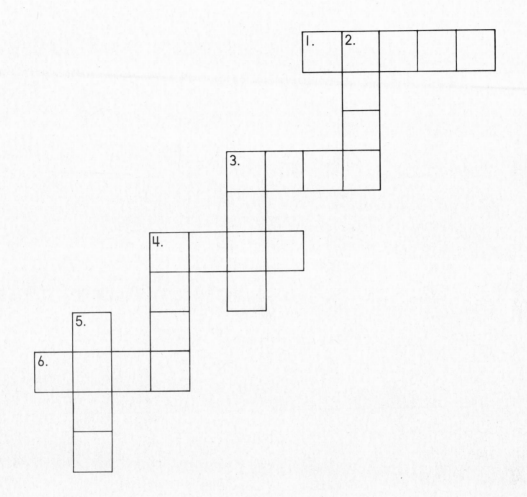

Across

1. The opposite of grown-up is ___.

3. The opposite of harsh is ___.

4. To crank or twist is to ___.

6. If we look for something we can ___ it.

Down

2. The opposite of front leg is ___ leg.

3. You think with your ___.

4. The opposite of tame is ___.

5. The opposite of mean is ___.

find   kind   hind   child   mind   wild   wind   mild

Pattern words with endings

On this page are some longer words with the **o** sound as in <u>go</u>, and the **i** sound as in <u>ride</u>. Most of them have **-er** or **-en** endings. Connect the words with the pictures.

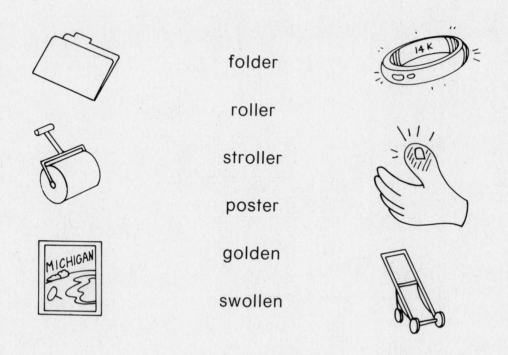

folder

roller

stroller

poster

golden

swollen

Choose the correct word. Write it in the blank.

roller   behind   posters   grinder

colder   mostly   holder

1. Use a pot _____ to lift the hot skillet off the stove.

2. The math quiz had _____ adding problems on it.

3. It is much _____ in March than it is in June.

4. Sue has many _____ hanging on her bedroom walls.

5. Mr. Carson used a _____ when he painted our house.

6. You get ground beef when you put meat into a _____ .

7. Mrs. Kelly told me to go and stand in line _____ you.

Pattern words

Tell if the sentences are <u>true</u> or <u>false</u>. <u>False</u> means <u>not</u> true.
Circle the correct word.

1. It is kind to help someone. . . . . true   false

2. The opposite of <u>tame</u> is <u>wild</u>. true   false

3. You smell with your mind. true   false

4. Rings can be made of gold. true   false

5. You can hold rainbows in your hand. . . . . true   false

6. An eighty-year-old man is called a child. . . . . true   false

7. A broken finger may be swollen. . . . . true   false

8. A colt is a horse. . . . . true   false

9. Most fathers like to ride in strollers. . . . . true   false

10. A blind man drives a car. . . . . true   false

11. The opposite of <u>most</u> is <u>least</u>. . . . . true   false

12. You try to find things that are lost. . . . . true   false

13. Egg yolks are yellow. . . . . true   false

14. On some roads you must pay tolls. . . . . true   false

15. You wind a real car to make it start. . . . . true   false

16. A ball can roll down a slope. . . . . true   false

17. The opposite of <u>cold</u> is <u>freezing</u>. . . . . true   false

18. It is easy to fold wood. . . . . true   false

19. A house can be sold. . . . . true   false

20. A story can be told to someone. . . . . true   false

-est ending meaning <u>most</u> or <u>least</u>

A way to make a word mean <u>more</u> or <u>less</u> is to use the ending **-er.**
The ending **-est** will make a word mean <u>most</u> or <u>least</u>. Read these.

My little brother is getting big .

I am bigger than he is.

My father is the biggest of us all.

Fill in the endings **-er** or **-est.**

1. Our cat is small .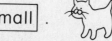

2. All her kittens are small_____ than she is.

3. This one kitten is the small_____ of all.

Write the word with the correct ending in the blank. Use **-er** or **-est.**

1. A puddle is not very deep .

2. A pond is _____ than a puddle.

3. A lake is _____ than a pond.

4. The sea is the _____ of all.

1. A man can walk fast .

2. A bike is _____ than walking.

3. A car is _____ than a bike.

4. An airplane is the _____.

-est ending meaning most or least

Read the questions. Underline the correct word or words.

1. Who is the oldest?

   child   father   brother   grandfather   mother   sister

2. What is the longest?

   fifteen miles   two miles   eighty miles   four miles

3. Where is it the coldest?

   stove   yard   freezer   window   oven   kitchen

4. Which tastes sweetest?

   salt   grapes   roll   mustard   liver   pie

5. When is it the hottest?

   spring   summer   March   winter   fall   Tuesdays

6. Which is the softest?

   pillow   penny   sand   wood   post   ground

7. What is the fastest?

   scooter   tractor   roller coaster   raft   buggy   stroller

8. Which is the smallest?

   puppy   cow   kitten   goldfish   ape   chicken

9. What is the sharpest?

   hammer   spoon   ruler   pinecone   rake   needle

10. What is the slowest?

    rabbit   snake   deer   mouse   raccoon   snail

Review of contractions

Look at the samples to see how to do these.

I've	has not	aren't →	a r e n o t
she's	it is	he's →	_ _ _ _
hasn't	I have	they've →	_ _ _ _ _ _
I'll	she will	you'll →	_ _ _ _ _ _
it's	I will	wasn't →	_ _ _ _ _
she'll	she is		

you have	you'll	we have →	w e ' v e
we will	wasn't	they will →	_ _ _ _ , _ _
you will	we've	that is →	_ _ _ _ , _
was not	didn't	you have →	_ _ _ ' _ _
we have	you've	she is →	_ _ _ ' _
did not	we'll		

Choose the contraction you need and write it on the line.

Pete_____dig with that old broken shovel.	can't
Sue_____done with her math problems.	isn't
_____ seen most of those old cartoons before.	Where's
_____ your sister going after school today?	We've
The vet will ask you _____ the matter with your pet.	what's
Our old car_____ running smoothly yesterday.	wasn't
Do you think_____ snow again before we go sledding?	I've
_____ got four mistakes that I have to correct.	it'll

Review of contractions

Look at the samples to see how to do these.

they've	had not	isn't ——→	i s n o t
he'll	he is	we'll ——→	_ _ _ _ _
there's	they will	there's ——→	_ _ _ _ _ _
hadn't	he will	mustn't ——→	_ _ _ _ _ _ _
he's	there is	she'll ——→	_ _ _ _ _ _ _
they'll	they have		

must not	aren't	it is ——→	i t ' s
cannot	that's	I will ——→	_ _ _
are not	mustn't	did not ——→	_ _ _ _ ' _
is not	it'll	I have ——→	_ ' _ _ _
that is	isn't	has not ——→	_ _ _ _ ' _
it will	can't		

Choose the contraction you need and write it on the line.

It _____ snowed this much in a long time.	he's
Joe says _____ not trying out for the baseball team.	hasn't
Please give me the glass _____ empty and clean.	that's
The crackers in that box _____ crispy anymore.	aren't
Dr. Watson says that _____ give you some pills.	he'll
_____ use our snow blower for the driveway.	they'll
Why _____ you come to the party last week?	you'll
_____ see waves as you walk along this shore.	didn't

168

Review of book

Read the questions. Circle the correct words.

Which of these are outside?

sidewalk	stones	carpet	clouds	snowflake	garden
oven	rainbow	sand dune	river	bathtub	hallway
waterfall	woods	campfire	lake	driveway	shrubs

What things have wheels?

tractor	hoe	airplane	van	fire truck	scooter
tire	skates	trike	throne	stroller	car
buggy	train	glue	bike	driveway	sled

Which of these can be alive?

mule	ape	walrus	fire	goldfish	kitty
wind	guppy	snake	eagle	colt	food
tadpole	water	chipmunk	insect	snow	whale

What things can be shaped like a square?

cake	boxes	pie	napkin	puzzle	tile
dime	window	globe	toaster	penny	frame
baking pan	star	cube	block	book	glove

What things are part of a kitchen?

food	shovel	thermos	clock	oven	freezer
toothpaste	stove	cookbook	flute	plates	timer
rolling pin	perfume	dishwasher	bowls	shampoo	chair

Review of book

Choose the correct word for each sentence. Write it on the line.

They're _____ the grapes in the sink.	rising
The rolls are _____ in the hot oven.	rinsing

Mike and Steve sometimes write notes in _____ .	cold
We get _____ from mines deep underground.	code
It's so _____ that the lake must be frozen.	coat
I left my rain _____ at home yesterday.	coal

Who is _____ care of the fish this weekend?	tacking
Everyone was _____ loudly at the same time.	taking
He's _____ the carpet down in the hallway.	talking

Long ago horses needed _____ posts.	hitching
The children were _____ in the woods.	hiking

We paid two dimes at the _____ booth.	told
When I was barefoot, I stubbed my big _____ .	toad
Who _____ you that Peggy was sick?	toe
A _____ has bumpy skin.	toll

His pet snake was _____ its skin.	shopping
Those old oak trees are _____ our yard.	shedding
Where were you _____ ?	shading

Review of book

Circle the word you need to finish the sentence.

---

1. Where you live is your........roof   home   school   garden

2. If you don't have any,
   you have ....some   plenty   one   none

3. Wood around a painting.......wall   canvas   frame   hook

4. Something that's not true......fact   line   told   lie

5. Things that belong to me are ...yours   mine   his   hers

6. If you're not on time, you're ...away   speedy   late   clock

7. A tool used for digging ....shovel   tractor   rake   hook

8. The opposite of frozen........swollen   melted   frosted   snow

9. It will become a frog ....colt   tadpole   toad   child

10. To talk softly ....scold   shout   whisper   agree

11. The deepest of these ....lake   pond   puddle   sea

12. The opposite of slowly ....safely   swiftly   easy   hardly

13. Bold sometimes means ....brave   lively   quickly   afraid

14. Four and two are.............eight   six   seven   five

15. You can find yolks in..........toes   bolts   eggs   cubes

16. Water you can wade in is .....square   deep   clear   shallow

17. To fix rope so it stays
    together ....tie   twine   glue   mend

18. You think with your ....skin   mind   spine   elbow

19. The opposite of love..........like   anger   hate   dislike

20. The quickest of these.........snail   walrus   goldfish   rabbit

Review of book

Look at the picture. Read the story. Then fill in the blanks in the sentences with words from the bottom of the page.

Yesterday Jimmy Benson became eight years_____. Dad and Mom

gave him two goldfish in a _____ as a gift. Jimmy _____

them Pete and Joe. Mom hung up streamers and Dad hung up the

_____ before the party began. There were _____

children at his party. Mr. Benson grilled _____ for

a picnic _____ outside. There was a big cake with _____

candles on it. All the children gave Jimmy_____. They played

many _____. The winners all got _____. Then Jimmy

said "Thank you" to everyone. Then they played with a _____

in the yard until it was time to go home. It was such fun!

old	hot dogs	games	balloons	ball	eight
five	lunch	bowl	named	gifts	prizes

Review of book

One word can sometimes mean two different things. Read the words and look at the pictures that show two meanings for the same word.

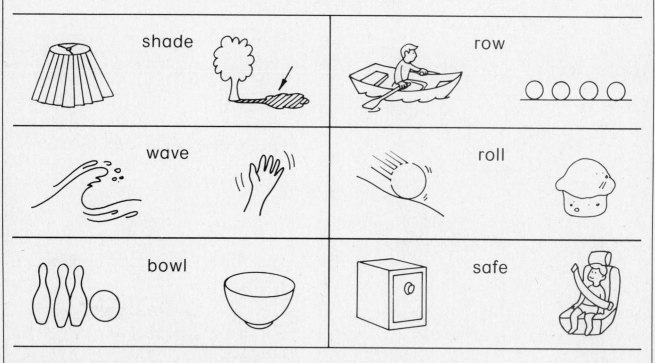

Fill in the word you need in these sentences. You will use each word two times.

safe   foot   close   waves   row

1. They were hoping to catch a fish at least one _____ long.

2. Mr. Hansen told us to _____ the windows before we go.

3. Most of the cash in the bank is kept in a _____ .

4. Who wants to go with me when I _____ across the lake?

5. My little brother _____ to everyone that he sees.

6. Who do you think lives _____ to Dr. Martin?

7. Whose _____ is it that keeps kicking mine under the desk?

8. What _____ do you want to sit in at the show?

9. There were twenty-foot _____ out at sea yesterday!

10. It's not _____ to mow the grass in your bare feet.

base	p l a y e d l o o k i n g	**because**	He sings because he is happy.
circle		**different**	
draw		**finish**	Finish counting. 1 2 3 _ _ _ _ _ _
line	Underline the word.	**page**	
picture		**question**	Why did she call?
remember	To remember is not to forget.	**sentence**	A sentence tells and it ends with a ▫
these	not this but these	**together**	Put the puzzle together.
write		**word**	2 ABC apple ←
vowels	a e i o u y	**consonants**	b c d f g h j k l m n p q r s t v w x y z